THE WORLD OF THE
HAPPY PEAR

To the wonderful people who are part of the Happy Pear story – friends, family, staff, customers and well-wishers. You help make our dreams possible. We are beyond grateful. It's been an incredible adventure so far, so thank you for your unending support.

THE WORLD OF THE
HAPPY PEAR

STEPHEN & DAVID FLYNN

Photograpy by ALISTAIR RICHARDSON

PENGUIN
IRELAND

PENGUIN IRELAND

UK | USA | Canada | Ireland | Australia
India | New Zealand | South Africa

Penguin Ireland is part of the Penguin Random House group of companies
whose addresses can be found at global.penguinrandomhouse.com.

Penguin
Random House
UK

First published 2016
001

Colour reproduction by Rhapsody Ltd
Printed in China

A CIP catalogue record for this book is available from the British Library

ISBN : 978–0–241–97553–4

www.greenpenguin.co.uk

MIX
Paper from
responsible sources
FSC   FSC® C018179
www.fsc.org

Penguin Random House is committed to a
sustainable future for our business, our readers
and our planet. This book is made from Forest
Stewardship Council® certified paper.

CONTENTS

WELCOME TO THE WORLD OF THE HAPPY PEAR!

It took us ten years to write our first book, *The Happy Pear*. We never really expected it to travel beyond our family and friends and the Happy Pear customers who had been asking for our recipes for years. We have been amazed with how far it has travelled outside our little bubble in Greystones and the wave it has made.

The positive reaction to the book has only increased our passion for what we do. We feel more inspired than ever to follow our dream of a happier, healthier, more connected world and spread the message of our three-word-manifesto – EAT MORE VEG!

In *The Happy Pear* we told the story of how we started: how we had been complete meat-heads growing up and how it was while travelling separately the year after we left college that we both decided to become vegetarian. Totally independently. Within the same week. True twin magic! We loved what eating a plant-based diet did for us and that translated into a passion for spreading the message when we got home to Ireland. We opened our veg shop in our hometown of Greystones in November 2004 and we've been having fun chasing our dreams since.

Many of our friends thought we were crazy with our little veg shop and clapped-out red van. But in the years since, more and more people have realized that what we put into our bodies has a real impact not just on weight but on everything from energy and concentration levels, to gut health, to making sure the body has the right mix of nutrients to function at its best.

Now we see many people who want to change, to be healthier and to feel better, but feel bombarded by so much info and don't necessarily know where to start. We want to say to people: don't panic! Getting healthier is not an all-or-nothing type thing but a series of stepping stones, making little changes that, over time, will have a real impact on your quality of life. Every step in the right direction will help you to be a better version of yourself. Eating more veg is easy, cheap and a habit worth cultivating. The Happy Pear way of eating is not a fad diet but something really straightforward. It is not focused on cutting out things but on eating more of the good stuff.

So, this book is all about encouraging you to eat more veg (by veg we really mean fruit, veg, beans, legumes and whole-grains). It will help inspire you to make changes you have wanted to make for years that will have a lasting effect on your health and your happiness.

As if that wasn't enough, we always said we wanted to start a food revolution, and by eating more veg you can join our revolution! If that sounds scary, it shouldn't. Eating more veg may sound like a simple thing, but we see it as something that can be the tipping point to so many other good things. Eating more veg means you are more likely to exercise, which will lead to the release of feel-good endorphins in your body and greater energy. You'll probably spend more time outside and meet more people, and generally have a better quality of life and a greater sense of being connected both to the environment and to other people.

We believe that having a sense of community and connection in your life is every bit as important as eating your veg. We all want to feel a sense of connection and this is why community is so vital. Healthy happy communities can help change the world for the better.

Our way of life is about following your dreams, doing more of what you love, eating good food that nourishes your body, getting out into the outdoors, having a laugh with friends, not taking things too seriously, moving your body every day as it feels good. It's not about perfection, it's not about being better than anyone else. It is very much about feeling good and creating habits that enrich your life and lead to a happier and more fulfilled you, and, leading from that, a better world for you, your kids, and your kids' kids.

Often someone's reason for not eating more healthily is that they can't imagine what they'll eat. They simply take meat out of the equation and don't feel very excited about eating what's left on the plate. And they worry that new stuff that they've never tried before will taste like 'cardboard' or 'rabbit food'. We can totally relate to that! In the days when we were meat-and-two-veg men, we had no idea of the world of tastes and foods that existed beyond our limited food choices and just how delicious healthy food could be.

We guarantee you that the food in this book will stand up taste-wise and will satisfy the most avid carnivore. We have 100 fab new recipes that we think are even better than those in our first book! We have focused more on quicker dinners. From our last book we saw how popular the burgers were, so we have a fantastic selection of veggie burgers (page 131–5) and barbecue cooking (pages 139–41) in our Mains section. Breakfast is one of our top three favourite meals, so we have some really great stuff there too! And, of course, because you definitely don't have to deprive yourself to be healthy, we have got lots of healthier desserts!

We've called our second book *The World of the Happy Pear* because we want to bring you into our world. By introducing you to members of our family, the Happy Pear team, our friends, neighbours and suppliers, and people who have done our health courses, we hope you will see how we live out our values. And we hope you will also see that eating more veg is for everybody. At the Happy Pear we love the amazing variety of people coming through our doors – from young vibrant health enthusiasts to eighty-year-olds getting their daily shot of wheatgrass or a smoothie. No matter what category you fit into, eating more veg improves your life!

Veg power!
Dave & Steve

BREAKFASTS

CHIA SEED PUDDING

This is a super-nutritious brekkie, packed with fibre, protein and omega-3s while being low in calories and fat! We never liked the texture of chia seed pudding until we came up with this recipe. The rice milk and banana give it a nice sweetness and the oats give it a bit more fibre and a change of texture. Another great brekkie if you are on the go – make it in a jar the night before and bring it with you to eat on the train or bus.

Mash the banana and the raspberries well. Put them into a jar or bowl, stir in all the other ingredients and leave to set for a couple of hours or overnight.

Sprinkle the top with some extra chia seeds and serve with fresh berries, bee pollen, cacao nibs, goji berries, fresh fruit or whatever you fancy!

SERVES 1–2

½ a banana

125g raspberries

2 tablespoons chia seeds

250ml rice milk

2 tablespoons oat flakes (porridge oats) – use gluten-free if you prefer, or leave them out altogether

GREEN POWER BOWL

This is a great summer brekkie idea and brill after exercise. It's basically a really thick smoothie that's covered with your favourite toppings or whatever you have to hand. If you can chop up the pineapple and freeze it the night before it'll taste a bit like eating ice-cream for breakfast – YUM! Put it into a jar or container for a brekkie on the go.

SERVES 2

1 ripe avocado
1 teaspoon spirulina/matcha green tea powder
3 tablespoons ground flax seeds
250g fresh or frozen pineapple or mango
400ml apple juice or coconut water
a handful of baby spinach

Scoop the avocado flesh out of its skin and put into a blender with all the other ingredients. Blend till smooth.

Top with whatever you like! Some suggestions are fresh mango, pomegranate seeds, your favourite nuts, goji berries, bee pollen, granola, cacao nibs, fresh berries, seeds … whatever you're into really!

ELSIE'S SUPER SMOOTHIE

Dave had the best drink he ever had in a health food shop in California. It was a green smoothie that cost $18 and he thought it was a mistake. It was the best mistake he ever tasted! For the last two years Dave and his daughters have been trying to reverse-engineer it; now they think they've cracked it!

Put all the ingredients into a blender and whiz till smooth. Top with some extra bee pollen.

MAKES ABOUT 1200ML

80g walnuts
50g goji berries
1 banana
2 heaped tablespoons cacao powder
1 tablespoon spirulina
2 tablespoons bee pollen (and some extra for topping)
1 litre water

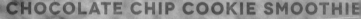

CHOCOLATE CHIP COOKIE SMOOTHIE

This is Dave's best shot at making a healthy brekkie smoothie that tastes as good as chocolate chip cookie dough ice-cream! We use water here to keep it light, but you can use milk of your choice instead.

Measure the water into a blender jug and add the vanilla extract. Soak the dates and cashew nuts in the water for 5 minutes. The orange zest can be a nice extra to add a zing to the flavour. Blend till smooth. Once blended, stir through the cacao nibs/dark chocolate chips, keeping them whole.

MAKES ABOUT 600ML

500ml water
¾ teaspoon vanilla extract
60g chopped dates
60g roasted cashew nuts
zest of 1 orange (optional)
3 tablespoons cacao nibs/dark chocolate chips

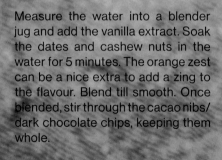

MINT CHOCOLATE CHIP SMOOTHIE

It's worth seeking out the peppermint oil for this recipe (it's also great added to superfood energy balls, see page 227, or a chocolate cake mixture). In this case it really makes this smoothie POP!

Put all the ingredients (except for the cacao nibs/dark chocolate chips) into a blender and blend until smooth. Once blended, mix through the cacao nibs/dark chocolate chips, keeping them whole.

MAKES ABOUT 600ML

60g cashew nuts
60g chopped dates
¾ teaspoon spirulina
a few drops of peppermint oil
500ml oat milk or milk of
  your choice
3 tablespoons cacao nibs/
  dark chocolate chips

FLU-BUSTER MOJITO SMOOTHIE

This super-healthy 'mojito' is sure to knock the socks off any cold or flu symptoms you have! It's a great pick-me-up and immune system booster.

Roll your lemon and grapefruit on a work surface (you always get more juice after rolling them). Squeeze the juice (removing any pips) and put into a blender jug.

Scoop out the avocado flesh from its skin and put into the blender along with the lemon, grapefruit and apple juice, and the mint leaves, removed from their stalks.

If you have a high-speed blender you can put the ginger in whole. If you have a regular blender, grate your ginger before adding. Blend the mixture well.

Serve with a couple of lemon slices and mint leaves in each glass.

MAKES ABOUT 650ML

juice of 1 lemon
juice of 1 grapefruit
1 ripe avocado
400ml apple juice
a good bunch of fresh mint
½ a thumb-size piece of
  fresh ginger
lemon slices and mint leaves,
  to garnish

HOMEMADE NON-DAIRY MILKS

Getting milk from a nut, seed or grain is much easier than from a cow. Homemade non-dairy milks taste great and are much cheaper than shop-bought versions.

We've only ever made almond, walnut, cashew, rice and oat milk. All these milks are raw, meaning they are full of enzymes. The science? Enzymes are biological catalysts, meaning that they make things happen in your body. Enzymes are really important for your body function and are only present in raw foods. Drinking these milks ensures we get lots of enzymes, good fats and hydration to get the day started! The nut milks are more expensive to make than oat or rice milk.

Try adding some vanilla extract, ground cinnamon or even nut butters to pimp up your milks. We keep these milks in bottles, jars or old containers in our fridge. They last for up to a week and can also be frozen.

RICE MILK

1 cup of cooked brown rice
4 cups of water

Blend the rice with the water until smooth. Sieve as before to give you a naturally sweet milk.

NUT MILK

1 cup of almonds, walnuts or
    cashews
3 cups of water

Soak the nuts overnight in water. The next morning drain them – they should have puffed up and got bigger.

Put the water and nuts into a blender and whiz until the mixture is super-smooth. Sieve as above, to give you a creamy, tasty milk.

HOMEMADE COCONUT YOGHURT

If you haven't tried coconut yoghurt yet, it's really worth tasting – wonderfully creamy, with a sense of decadent richness! It goes great anywhere you'd use yoghurt, also as a snack over fresh apple with some almond butter, or on top of our granola (see page 22).

You can control how thick your yoghurt will be by the proportion of coconut cream to coconut liquid you use from the tin. For example, if you want a thick yoghurt, use mostly the cream and omit the coconut liquid from the tin; if you want a runnier yoghurt, use everything in the tin.

Pour the coconut milk into a bowl and whisk until smooth and uniform. You are looking for a smooth homogenous texture – in some cases you may have to heat and cool the coconut milk to reach this homogeneous uniform texture. Ensure it has cooled to below 37° before adding the culture. Add the maple syrup/agave syrup. Next add your culture of choice: whisk in the store-bought coconut yoghurt gently, or add the contents of your probiotic capsules. Mix well.

Pour the coconut milk into any sterilized jars (see page 259 for details) and screw on the lids. Place in a warm airing cupboard or a preheated oven – put the oven on the lowest temperature possible and leave the door slightly open. Leave for 24 hours without disturbing. Ideally the temperature is between 30 and 40°C.

Place the set yoghurt in the fridge for at least 6 hours. The yoghurt will become thicker as it chills. After this stage, you might find that the mixture has separated, with a yellowish, translucent layer at the bottom and a thicker white layer on top. Stir to recombine, or scoop off the top layer for thicker coconut yoghurt.

Keep your coconut yoghurt refrigerated and use within 1 week.

MAKES 400ML

- 1 x 400ml tin of coconut milk (full-fat if you want a creamier yoghurt)
- 1 teaspoon maple syrup/ agave syrup
- 2 tablespoons shop-bought coconut yoghurt or 2 capsules of probiotic culture*

* You can get probiotic capsules in any health food shop. For this recipe make sure your capsules contain one of these strains: *Lactobacillus bulgaricus*, *Streptococcus thermophilus*, *Bifidobacterium lactis* or *Lactobacillus acidophilus*.

COCONUT YOGHURT POTS THREE WAYS

A really tasty way to use your homemade coconut yoghurt – great for a brekkie or snack on the go! Just get some clean jars (or use a glass) and assemble. You can use any type of yoghurt, so don't feel like this only works with coconut.

POMEGRANATE SEEDS AND HONEYED PISTACHIOS

1 pomegranate
a small handful of shelled
  pistachios
1 tablespoon honey/agave syrup
200ml coconut yoghurt, or
  yoghurt of choice

Cut the pomegranate in half. Put one half face down on a chopping board and bang the back until the seeds fall out. Repeat with the other half. Drain any extra juice from the seeds and remove any white pith. Put the seeds into each of your two jars as the base layer.

Toast the pistachios in a dry frying pan until they start to colour – about 5 minutes. Remove from the heat, transfer to a bowl and add the honey. Stir through.

Fill your jars three-quarters of the way up with the yoghurt (on top of the pomegranate seeds), and top with the honeyed toasted pistachios.

FRESH BERRIES AND GRANOLA

50g fresh berries of choice
200ml coconut yoghurt, or
  yoghurt of choice
50g granola (see page 22)

Put a mixture of fresh berries (try raspberries, blueberries, strawberries, goji berries, blackberries . . .) into each of your two jars as the base layer.

Fill your jars with the yoghurt (on top of the berries), and top with the granola.

GREEN POWER BREKKIE POT

200ml green power bowl
  (see page 15)
200ml coconut yoghurt, or
  yoghurt of choice
50g granola (see page 22)

Divide the granola between the two jars. Top each with half the yoghurt. Finally top with your green power bowl mix. You can garnish with bee pollen if you like.

FLUFFY, CRUNCHY GRANOLA

This is one of the nicest granolas we have ever eaten or made, and we have eaten a lot – the first time we made this we thought it was a bit like eating sweet crunchy clouds! Use gluten-free oat flakes if you like.

Preheat the oven to 140°C/275°F/gas mark 1.

Mix all the dry ingredients together in a large bowl.

Melt the coconut oil by heating it in a small pan, then leave it to cool slightly. Put the honey/maple syrup/agave syrup into a bowl and add the coconut oil.

Pour the wet mixture into the bowl of dry ingredients and mix thoroughly.

Lay out the mixture in a thin even layer on two large baking trays. Put them into the oven and bake for about an hour. You can bake them longer if you prefer more of a crunch – no more than 10 extra minutes, though, as you don't want the granola to burn!

While your granola is baking, assemble your dried fruit in a bowl and add the ground flax seeds.

Once the granola is baked, leave it to cool on the baking tray for 20 minutes, then transfer to a clean mixing bowl and stir in the dried fruit, ground flax and the fancy stuff.

Goes great with milk or yoghurt (see our coconut yoghurt recipe on page 19), or to have on its own as a healthy snack throughout the day.

MAKES ABOUT 800G

400g oat flakes (to make it grain-free use rolled quinoa flakes)

50g flaked almonds (chopped Brazil nuts or raw cashews also go great!)

50g sunflower seeds

50g pumpkin seeds

50g desiccated coconut

a pinch of sea salt

120g coconut oil

90g honey/maple syrup/ agave syrup

100g dried fruit of choice (e.g. currants, raisins, chopped dates, chopped dried apricots, chopped prunes)

50g ground flax seeds

30g of fancy stuff (e.g. goji berries, freeze-dried strawberries or raspberries)

OVERNIGHT BIRCHER MUESLI

This recipe is really easy. You can have everything done the night before and just grab it running out the door in the morning – it looks very nice in a Kilner jar if you have one. It will keep for two days in the fridge.

Soaking oats overnight makes them sweeter and easier to digest. They are loaded with fibre to boost your digestion and immune system. Chia seeds add a nice texture as well as boosting the nutritional profile of this dish massively, especially omega-3, protein and fibre.

The night before, put the oats, raisins, goji berries, chia and pumpkin seeds into a bowl or container and mix. Add the rice milk, cover and put into the fridge.

In the morning, add your toppings – here are some ideas:

- blueberries • raspberries • banana • grated apple/pear
- yoghurt • bee pollen • granola

SERVES 2–3

100g oats
2 tablespoons raisins
1 tablespoon goji berries
2 tablespoons chia seeds
1 tablespoon pumpkin seeds
400ml rice milk

CREAMY COCONUT QUINOA 'PORRIDGE'

With porridge being our go-to comfort food it was hard for us to try making it with other grains – we felt like we were cheating on our lifelong friend the oat flake! This super-tasty brekkie will help you spring out of bed and it's particularly good on the weekend or after training, as it is richer than the usual porridge. It goes great with a good dollop of the citrus, goji and chia marmalade (see page 33), or raspberry chia jam (see page 33).

Put all the ingredients into a pot, put on a high heat and stir regularly. Bring to the boil, then turn down to a low to medium heat, and stir regularly. It should take about 10–15 minutes to cook.

Be careful to leave a little bit of moisture in the quinoa so that the porridge gets creamy and does not dry out. Remove the cardamom pods, cinnamon, star anise and vanilla pod before serving.

SERVES 2–3

600ml rice milk
1 x 400ml tin of full-fat coconut milk
250g quinoa
5 cardamom pods
1 cinnamon stick
1 star anise (optional)
½ a vanilla pod
a pinch of salt

QUINOA AND FLAX PANCAKES

We first made these pancakes with our friend the lovely Roz Purcell. They are super-tasty, packed full of protein, complex carbs and good fats, and have the added benefit of being gluten- and dairy-free.

In a high-speed blender or coffee grinder, blend the uncooked quinoa and flax seeds together until they reach a flour-like consistency (they do blend in some regular domestic blenders but not all!). Add the rest of the ingredients, except the oil, and whiz together.

Pour a tiny dash of oil into a non-stick frying pan, mix it around the pan and wipe away with a piece of kitchen paper to remove any extra fat. Put the pan on a high heat and allow it to heat up for a few minutes.

Pour in a dollop of your pancake batter and spread it out evenly in the pan. Turn the heat down to medium. Once the edges start to cook and the centre starts to develop holes or bubbles, flip the pancake over and cook the other side until it gets light brown. Put your cooked pancake on a plate and cover it with a tea towel to keep warm. Make the rest of your pancakes the same way, until the batter is used up.

TIP: If the batter starts to get too thick, add a little more rice milk to thin it out.

MAKES ABOUT 10 SMALL PANCAKES

125g quinoa (uncooked)
2 tablespoons whole flax seeds
250ml rice milk
1 teaspoon vanilla extract
¾ of a medium-size banana
2 tablespoons honey
a pinch of salt
a little oil for cooking

Toppings:
fresh fruit of your choice
yoghurt
honey

PINK PANCAKES WITH RED GRAPEFRUIT GUACAMOLE

These tasty, healthy pancakes have the benefits of being gluten-free, dairy-free, low in fat, low in calories, and high in fibre, vitamins, minerals and antioxidants. All in all a super start for brekkie or a fun dinner.

You want to extract all the bright purply-pink juice from the beetroot, so grate it into a bowl using the fine side of the grater, making sure to catch the juice. Take a second bowl and squeeze the grated beetroot flesh over it so the juice comes out. Wear a glove, as the juice stains and is hard to wash off! Discard the flesh. You can use a strainer to strain the last bit of the flesh and juice from the first bowl into the second so you capture all the juice.

Put the juice and all the other pancake ingredients (except the oil) into a blender and blend till smooth. Alternatively, if you have a stick blender, add all the ingredients to the bowl of beetroot juice and blend in the bowl.

To cook your pancakes, heat your pan till it gets nice and hot. Pour in a small amount of oil and spread to cover the base. Wipe off excess oil with kitchen paper, so only a tiny coating remains on the pan. Turn down to a medium heat.

Pour in some batter, enough to make a small thin pancake. When bubbles start to form in the middle and the edges start to firm up, turn and cook the other side. Put your cooked pancake on a plate and cover with a tea towel to keep it warm. Make the rest of your pancakes the same way, until the batter is used up.

To make the guacamole, peel the grapefruit using a knife so you leave out the bitter pith – the thin white layer between the skin and the flesh. Cut the segments out of the membrane and cut each segment into two or three pieces. Chop the avocado flesh into chunks.

Put the chopped grapefruit and avocado into a bowl with all the other ingredients except the chilli flakes, and mix lightly with a fork. Leave it so it's not too mushy and there is lots of texture.

Put some of the guacamole on top of each pancake, garnish with the chilli flakes, and enjoy!

MAKES ABOUT 10 SMALL PANCAKES

100g fresh beetroot

200g buckwheat flour

350ml rice milk

½ teaspoon salt

3–4 teaspoons honey (depending on how sweet you want it)

⅓ of a ripe banana

zest of ½ a medium-size orange (organic if possible, as non-organic ones have wax on the skin)

125g raspberries

oil for frying

For the red grapefruit guacamole:

2 red grapefruit

1 ripe avocado

a handful of fresh coriander

¼ of a red onion, chopped finely

a pinch of freshly ground black pepper

a pinch of salt

a pinch of ground chilli

1 teaspoon ground cumin

chilli flakes, to garnish

A non-stick pan is essential for this recipe. Otherwise you will need to use more oil to make sure the pancakes don't stick.

CORN FRITTERS WITH AN AVOCADO SALSA

A great brunch served with a few slices of toast and some beans, this is a meal to be reckoned with! The avocado salsa really complements the fritters. Polenta flour is worth seeking out to have in your store cupboard. Once made, the fritter mix will keep for a few days in your fridge and can be frozen. Hummus goes great with these too.

Drain the sweetcorn and rinse it thoroughly. Peel the garlic, and deseed and finely chop the red chilli (keep the seeds in if you like it hot!), together with the garlic and scallions. Put into a blender.

Add the rest of the fritter ingredients (apart from the extra polenta flour and the oil) to the blender and whiz for about a minute, until they form a lumpy but cohesive texture. Divide the mix into 4–6 balls and flatten each into a patty shape.

Before frying, put a couple of tablespoons of polenta flour on a plate and roll the fritters in it to dry them out.

Put a tablespoon of oil into a pan and heat it for 1 minute on a high heat, then reduce to a medium heat and fry the fritters on either side until golden brown. It should take about 5 minutes to cook a fritter, and we cook them two at a time.

Roughly chop the tomato and avocado flesh into cubes and chop the coriander roughly. Put these into a large bowl with the rest of the salsa ingredients and mix well.

Serve the fritters with a dollop of salsa. Hummus is nice on them too.

MAKES 4–6 FRITTERS

For the fritters:
1 x 340g tin of sweetcorn
2 cloves of garlic
½ a red chilli
3 scallions
2 tablespoons ground flax seeds
8 tablespoons polenta flour, plus extra for coating
juice of ½ a lime
1 teaspoon salt
½ teaspoon freshly ground black pepper
1 teaspoon ground coriander
1 teaspoon ground cumin
1 tablespoon oil

For the salsa:
1 tomato
1 avocado
a few sprigs of fresh coriander
juice of 1 lime
½ teaspoon salt
¼ teaspoon freshly ground black pepper
½ teaspoon dried chilli flakes

RASPBERRY AND ALMOND GLUTEN-FREE MUFFINS

Addictive and delicious – the first time Steve made these, he ate four by accident! They are like a light, fluffy, almondy flapjack muffin, with the sweetness and sharpness of raspberries cutting through. Try them with some homemade coconut yoghurt (see page 19) on the side.

Preheat the oven to 160°C/325°F/gas mark 3. Line a muffin tray with 12 paper muffin cases.

In a small bowl, mix the ground flax seeds and water to make 'flax eggs' (see page 253) and leave to sit while you prepare the rest of the ingredients.

Put the oats, ground almonds, baking powder and bicarbonate of soda into a large bowl and mix well.

Melt the coconut oil by heating in a small pan and add it (or the vegetable oil) to the bowl of dry ingredients along with the agave syrup/date syrup, vanilla extract and 'flax eggs'. Mix thoroughly.

Stir in three-quarters of the flaked almonds and three-quarters of the raspberries, reserving the rest for later.

Get your muffin tray and pour the mixture into the paper cases, ensuring you have the same amount in each one. Scatter the remaining flaked almonds over the top, then bake in the oven for 25 minutes. Once cooked, remove and leave to cool in the tin.

Place the remaining raspberries on top. These muffins will keep for up to 3 days.

MAKES 12

2 tablespoons ground flax seeds
6 tablespoons water
180g oats
160g ground almonds
1 teaspoon baking powder
½ teaspoon bicarbonate of soda
150g coconut oil/140ml
  vegetable oil
150g agave syrup/date syrup
2 teaspoons vanilla extract
20g flaked almonds
125g raspberries

NUT AND SEED POWER LOAF

This sweet fibre-powered gluten-free bread will make you and your bowels big and strong! It will keep you full, well-fuelled and ready for any activity. Psyllium husk powder is essential for this recipe, as it is the main binder. If you can't find it in health food shops, order it online – it's not expensive. This bread is great on its own and is so tasty when toasted!

Preheat the oven to 180°C/350°F/gas mark 4, and line a 450g loaf tin with baking parchment.

Mix the psyllium husk powder and water in a bowl and set aside for 5 minutes, until it develops a thick, gel-like consistency.

Put all the other ingredients into a food processor. Pulse until the nuts are chopped and the mix is an even texture, with no big pieces, but do not allow it to become a flour or a paste.

Put the nut and seed mix into a large bowl, and add the psyllium mix. Give it a good stir with your hands. Pour into your prepared tin and place in the oven.

After 45 minutes, take the loaf from the oven. Remove the bread from the loaf tin, peel off the baking parchment, turn it upside down, then put it back into the tin. Be careful handling the very hot bread: use a tea towel! Put the loaf back into the oven to bake for a further 45 minutes.

Remove from the oven and let it cool (about 2 hours) in the tin before turning it out and slicing. Be patient – it needs to cool properly, otherwise it'll crumble. Enjoy!

TIP: Best stored wrapped in a kitchen towel in the fridge – it will keep for up to a week like this. It also freezes well.

MAKES A 450G LOAF

2 tablespoons psyllium husk powder
300ml water
100g sunflower seeds
100g pumpkin seeds
100g almonds/walnuts/cashew nuts
50g flax seeds/chia seeds
50g currants/raisins
50g chopped dates
2 apples, grated
100g gluten-free oats
1 teaspoon sea salt

CITRUS, GOJI AND CHIA MARMALADE

This is a rocking little marmalade that is sugar-free and packed full of superfoods. It's also super-simple to make and requires no cooking! Great on toast, porridge, pancakes or simply eaten off a spoon! Chia seeds are a great source of omega-3 EFAs (essential fatty acids), so great for brain function and blood flow. Try to use organic, unwaxed fruits if possible. This keeps for about a week in a sealed jar in the fridge, and freezes well too.

Using a very fine zester, zest a good strip of each of the three fruits (you need 1 compact teaspoon full of zest altogether).

Peel the grapefruit and orange, remove any pips, and pulse in a blender along with the honey, zest and salt.

Add the goji berries, chia seeds, ground ginger and a squeeze of lemon juice to the blended citrus mix and leave to soak and soften for about 15 minutes.

Pulse the mixture again – we like to leave it a bit lumpy rather than smooth.

MAKES 200G

1 lemon
1 grapefruit
1 orange
3 tablespoons thick honey
a pinch of salt
80g goji berries
3 tablespoon chia seeds
½ teaspoon ground ginger

RASPBERRY CHIA JAM

If you have been looking for a sugar-free jam that takes five minutes to make, look no further! If you prefer strawberry, blueberry or blackberry jam, simply use these fruits instead of the raspberries here. It keeps for about a week in the fridge.

Mash the raspberries with a fork or blend them in a blender. Add the chia seeds and honey and mix well with a spoon to avoid clumps and to get a consistent taste.

Spoon into a jar and leave to set in the fridge for an hour.

Enjoy on toast or on pancakes or simply as a topping for your porridge – definitely try it on the coconut quinoa porridge (see page 24)!

MAKES 200G

125g raspberries
2 tablespoons chia seeds
3 teaspoons thick honey

PAN-FRIED KALE, ASPARAGUS, OYSTER MUSHROOM AND CHILLI TOASTIE

A really tasty brunch recipe, full of flavour, and with the sun-dried tomato pesto and avocado it will knock your socks off! Dave often makes the kale part of this for dinner – it is quite a robust recipe.

First make the dressing by whisking all the ingredients together in a cup or jug. Set aside.

Remove the kale stalks and cut the leaves into bite-size chunks. Place in a large bowl.

Cut the woody ends off the asparagus and discard. Slice the remainder of each spear into three. Add to the kale in the bowl.

Cut the mushrooms into bite-size pieces, keeping them separate from the other veg. Peel the onion, garlic and ginger. Chop the onion and put into a bowl. Finely dice the garlic and chilli, grate the ginger, and put all together into a separate bowl. Keep the chilli seeds in if you like it hot!

Heat a large frying pan for 1 minute on a high heat and add 4 tablespoons of the dressing, together with the onions. Fry for 3 minutes, stirring regularly. Add the garlic, ginger and chilli with another 2 tablespoons of the dressing, and fry for a further 3 minutes.

Now add the oyster mushrooms, along with the rest of the dressing and fry for 4 minutes. The mushrooms will absorb all the remaining dressing.

Finally, add the kale and the asparagus and cook for a further 3 minutes, stirring regularly. Stir in the sesame seeds.

This goes great over toasted sourdough bread spread with sun-dried tomato pesto. As a final touch, we love it with a couple of thin slices of avocado and a sprinkle of alfalfa sprouts. Yum!

SERVES 2

300g kale
½ a bunch of asparagus
  (about 10 spears)
150g oyster or any mushroom
  (oyster are worth seeking out!)
1 red onion
3 cloves of garlic
a thumb-size piece of
  fresh ginger
1 red chilli
2 tablespoons sesame seeds

For the dressing:
4 tablespoons tamari
juice of 2 lemons or limes
3 tablespoons water
1½ tablespoons honey/maple
  syrup/agave syrup

To serve:
sourdough bread
1 tub of sun-dried tomato pesto
1 ripe avocado
alfalfa sprouts

GREEK DAKOS

Dakos is a type of bruschetta using toasted crunchy bread that is rehydrated with olive oil and juices from fresh tomatoes, then topped with fresh feta, olive tapenade and some oregano leaves, if you have any. These are really tasty little fellas that will leave you wanting more!

Toast the slices of bread until they are really crunchy.

Make a quick tapenade by finely chopping together the pitted olives and a few of the oregano/dill leaves and adding a squeeze of fresh lemon juice. Leave some herb leaves aside for the topping.

Grate the tomatoes into a bowl.

Drizzle 1 tablespoon of olive oil on top of each slice. Top with the grated tomato and crumble over the feta. Layer on some oregano or dill leaves and finally top each slice with the olive tapenade and a few more herb leaves to garnish.

SERVES 4

4 large slices of lovely bread
100g pitted black olives
a small sprinkle of fresh oregano/
    dill leaves
a squeeze of fresh lemon juice
2 tomatoes
4 tablespoons olive oil
150g feta cheese

BAKED BEEF TOMATO AND EGG WITH THYME AND CHIVES

This is one of our chef Claire's recipes. It's a really nice, simple brekkie that looks and tastes great, a good one for the weekend or for when you have a little more time (thyme!). It's important to use large beef tomatoes, otherwise you'll need to draw off some egg white to prevent spillage.

Preheat the oven to 170°C/325°F/gas mark 3.

Remove the leaves from the thyme and finely chop. Cut each tomato in half and scoop out the inside, then sprinkle with a little of the chopped thyme (and half the chives, if using). Brush the inside of each tomato with olive oil and lightly season inside with salt and pepper.

Using a circular cutter (or a knife), cut a 3–4cm diameter circle out of the centre of each slice of bread (this will stop the tomatoes falling over when baking in the oven). Brush the slices of bread and the cut-out circles with olive oil and lightly season with salt and pepper.

Place a tomato half in each circular hole in the bread, crack an egg inside, sprinkle with the rest of the fresh herbs, season and drizzle ½ teaspoon of oil on top. Put the small bread circle 'soldier' beside the tomato on the slice of bread.

Put on a baking tray and bake for 10–15 minutes, depending on how you like your eggs.

SERVES 4

5 stalks of fresh thyme

2 large beef tomatoes

1 tablespoon chopped chives (optional)

olive oil

salt and freshly ground black pepper

4 slices of bread, cut 2cm thick (any rustic bread – sourdough is always nice)

4 eggs, preferably free-range or organic

GREENS, CHEDDAR AND CHERRY TOMATO FRITTATA

This is a really simple tasty brekkie that works great as an easy weekend brunch. We've made this lots of times using young spring nettles that we get from the garden to accompany spinach or other greens. Cooked nettle leaves turn into delicate greens, with a flavour like mild spinach and a unique texture. Don't feel limited – you can replace the listed veg with whatever you have or whatever you like!

Preheat the oven to 200°C/400°F/gas mark 6.

Slice the scallions and halve the cherry tomatoes. Destalk the kale/nettles if using and roughly chop all the greens.

Put the oil into a standard frying pan that can go into the oven, then add the scallions and cherry tomatoes and cook for 5 minutes on a medium heat. Add the greens and leave to wilt for a few minutes.

Meanwhile, crack the eggs into a large bowl and whisk along with half the cheese and the salt and pepper. Pour the egg mix into the pan of vegetables and cook until the base and sides have set (around 5 minutes). Sprinkle the remaining cheese on top and place the pan in the oven or under the grill until the top sets and turns golden brown – about 5 minutes.

SERVES 6

6–8 scallions

200g cherry tomatoes

200g fresh greens – spinach, chard, kale, young nettles

2 tablespoons oil

10 eggs, preferably free-range or organic

150g grated Cheddar cheese/ crumbled feta cheese/ goat's cheese

1 teaspoon salt

1 teaspoon freshly ground black pepper

VEGAN FULL IRISH

Every Christmas morning extended family members cook a big hearty – meaty! – full Irish brekkie, and for the last thirteen years we have looked on while eating porridge. Much as we love our porridge, we want to get in on the act, so here is our version to share with them this year! It takes a bit of time, but it's tasty and fun to do! ☺ Ideally serve these with homemade beans (page 49), as they add moisture.

VEGAN SAUSAGES

MAKES 14

½ a medium onion

3 cloves of garlic

4 tablespoons oil

100g creamed coconut concentrate

1 x 400g tin of pinto beans, well-drained

2 tablespoons tamari/soy sauce

2 tablespoons tomato purée

1 teaspoon ground coriander

½ teaspoon smoked paprika

½ teaspoon freshly ground black pepper

1½ teaspoons salt

4 tablespoons ground flax seeds

90g oats

65ml water

1 teaspoon dried thyme or sage (optional)

polenta (or other flour), for dusting

These actually really taste like sausages. It's important that you make the mix dry enough so that they take shape easily. We also found that if you coat them in polenta they are easier to work with and hold their shape better. A little dried thyme or sage is a good addition if you have either.

Peel and finely chop the onion and garlic. Put them into a non-stick pan on a high heat with 2 tablespoons of oil, and cook until the onion softens and starts to brown – about 3 minutes.

While the onion and garlic are cooking, finely chop the coconut cream concentrate. Put it into a food processor along with the rest of the ingredients (apart from the polenta and the rest of the oil). Once the onion and garlic are cooked, add them to the processor and blend everything together until the mix is reasonably smooth but still has some texture. You don't want it becoming like a hummus!

Dust your hands with polenta to stop the mix sticking, then take small scoops of the mix and roll them into sausage shapes about 10cm long and 2cm in diameter. Dust each sausage with polenta so they are easier to roll.

Fry the sausages in the remaining 2 tablespoons of oil on a medium heat until nicely browned on each side.

TEMPEH RASHERS

MAKES ABOUT 12

1 teaspoon smoked paprika
2 cloves of garlic, crushed
2 tablespoons tamari/soy sauce
1 tablespoon tomato purée
1 tablespoon cider vinegar
4 tablespoons oil
2 tablespoons water
1 teaspoon honey/agave syrup
150g fresh tempeh

Lovely strong salted and smoked flavours infuse the tempeh to create that umami rasher-like flavour. These are quick, easy to make and taste great.

Make the marinade by blending all the ingredients – apart from the tempeh and 2 tablespoons of oil – until super-smooth, using a stick blender or food processor, or a bowl and a whisk.

Slice the tempeh into very thin slivers, rasher size, about ½cm thick, and place in a bowl. Spread the marinade evenly over the sliced tempeh and leave to sit for 5–10 minutes. Marinate longer for a deeper flavour.

Put a non-stick frying pan on a medium heat with the remaining 2 tablespoons of oil and add the marinated tempeh, turning it over so that each side is lovely and crispy and grizzly and packed full of flavour!

TOFU SCRAMBLED EGG

MAKES ABOUT 4 SMALL PORTIONS

200g firm block of tofu
¼ of a small onion
1 clove of garlic
2 tablespoons oil
2 tablespoons tamari/soy sauce
½ teaspoon ground turmeric

We have to come clean: the taste isn't much like scrambled egg! But it does look the part, and it's really tasty and goes great with beans, toast and the tempeh rashers.

Drain the tofu and discard any extra liquid. Then chop it into small bite-size squares, put them into a bowl and mash with a fork.

Peel and finely dice the onion and garlic. Put a frying pan on a high heat, add the oil, and fry the onions and garlic for about 2 minutes. Add the tofu, tamari/soy sauce and turmeric and fry for 4–5 minutes, until the tofu looks nice and yellow. Voilà: scrambled eggs, vegan style!

BEANS ON TOAST

This is a really simple recipe that takes about twenty minutes and is the backbone of a brunch for many! Great just with toast or as part of our vegan full Irish. Will keep for about three days in the fridge and freezes well.

Peel and finely chop the onions and garlic.

Heat the oil (or a splash of water) in a large pan over a medium heat and add the onions and garlic. Cook for 5–10 minutes, stirring, until the onions are translucent.

Add the passata and simmer for a few minutes to release the sweetness of the onions.

Add the beans, tamari/soy sauce, apple cider vinegar, honey/maple syrup/liquid sweetener, salt, black pepper, cumin, chilli powder and bay leaves (if using) and continue to simmer for 10 minutes more. Finally, taste and see if it needs more seasoning.

Serve on toast or fresh crusty bread.

SERVES 4

2 medium onions

2 cloves of garlic

2 tablespoons oil

1 x 680g jar of passata

2 x 400g tins of borlotti beans or mixed beans

3 tablespoons tamari/ soy sauce

3 tablespoons apple cider vinegar

3 tablespoons honey/maple syrup/liquid sweetener

2 teaspoons salt

½ teaspoon freshly ground black pepper

2 teaspoons ground cumin

½ teaspoon chilli powder

2 bay leaves (optional)

SOUPS

HOW TO MAKE VEG STOCK

People think stock is complicated but it is just getting flavours into water – kinda like making tea! We sometimes use powdered ready-made stocks, which serve a purpose and are practical, but homemade stock is wholesome, more flavoursome and cheaper than buying it.

Instead of giving you a recipe to follow to the letter, here are our veg stock basics. As you can see, it's much simpler than you thought!

WHAT TO USE IN YOUR STOCK

There is no need to buy any fresh vegetables. Making stock is a great way to use veg trimmings that would otherwise be tossed into the bin. Indeed, it can be a mix of all the veg in the bottom of your fridge that is past its best – perfect for rubbery carrots, wilting scallions, half a soft onion, a few random cloves of garlic in the fridge door, some sad-looking herbs . . . just make sure there's no rot or mould on anything!

In our kitchens every morning, we have all sorts of veg peelings, seeds, spices, roots and leaves all in pots bubbling away, infusing their flavours into the water. Things we usually include are carrot tops, onion skins (use sparingly), garlic skins, garlic cloves and herb stalks, as well as seeds from pumpkins and squashes. (We've never done this but friends say freezing veg trimmings and scraps in an airtight container or bag is a great habit to get into, and then you have a base when you are ready to simmer a pot of stock.)

We also add herbs and mellow spices, e.g. bay leaves, cinnamon sticks, mustard seeds, juniper berries, fresh garlic, coriander seeds and peppercorns.

Seaweeds are great to include, too, as they will really amp up the nutritional and mineral element of your soup. Kombu works particularly well.

HOW TO MAKE YOUR STOCK

Put all your ingredients into a large pot with enough water to cover well and give you as much stock liquid as you desire, bring to the boil, then reduce to a gentle simmer. An hour is usually enough time for the flavours to infuse into the water, though the longer you leave it the more flavoursome and concentrated the stock will get.

Take the pot off the stove and remove all the flavouring ingredients with a slotted spoon. Or pour everything through a colander into another large pot. Discard the bits in the colander. Then set a strainer over a big bowl and pour the stock through.

Divide the stock between storage containers, cool completely, then put into the fridge or freezer.

BEETROOT: this will turn your stock pink, so best avoided unless you want a pink soup!

CRUCIFEROUS VEG: we never use cruciferous veg (e.g. broccoli, cauliflower, cabbage), since these contain sulphur and can give off too strong a flavour, making the broth bitter and unpleasant smelling.

STRONG SPICES: we don't usually include any strong spices unless we are making a spicy soup, so it's nearly always no chilli, curry powder, turmeric or cumin seed.

POTATOES: these will make your stock cloudy and starchy.

ONION SKINS: mentioned left, but avoid adding too many onion skins as they will make your stock brown.

ROSEMARY: this herb can be very dominant, so go gently with it.

MEDITERRANEAN VEG: we never use veg like peppers, aubergines or courgettes, as they do not really break down or add any flavours to the stock.

BELLY HUG LENTIL SOUP

Nothing nourishes you like a cooked red lentil, and this is one of those soups that's guaranteed to please. This soup freezes well, so it's worth doubling the recipe and storing some in the freezer for days when you need a belly hug! Note: This is a chunky soup, but if you prefer smoother soups just blend it at the end.

Peel and roughly chop the onion, garlic and ginger. Peel the celeriac. Chop the celeriac and carrots into small bite-size pieces so that they will cook quickly.

Get a large pot, add the oil and fry the onion, garlic and ginger on a high heat for 4 minutes, or until the onions are starting to brown and the garlic is turning golden. Add the carrots and celeriac together with the salt and mix well. Put the lid on the pot, turn the heat down to medium and leave to cook for 5 minutes, stirring occasionally.

Add the chopped tomatoes, lentils, stock, curry powder, black pepper and cinnamon. Stir well, put the lid on, and bring to the boil, then reduce to a simmer and leave to cook for 30 minutes, stirring regularly to make sure the lentils don't stick to the bottom of the pot.

Check the seasoning and add more salt and pepper if necessary. Remove from the heat. Add the spinach just before serving.

SERVES 4–6

1 medium onion

2 cloves of garlic

a thumb-size piece of fresh ginger

200g celeriac

2 medium carrots

2 tablespoons oil

2 teaspoons salt

1 x 400g tin of good-quality chopped tomatoes

200g split red lentils

2 litres vegetable stock or water

2 tablespoons medium curry powder

½ teaspoon freshly ground black pepper

½ teaspoon ground cinnamon

100g baby spinach or similar greens, to serve

MOROCCAN GRILLED RED PEPPER, CHICKPEA, ROASTED GARLIC AND HARISSA SOUP

This chunky, hefty red soup is full of flavour and spice. Harissa is a chilli paste (see recipe on page 182). Great for dinner or lunch, with some toasted wholemeal pittas.

Preheat the oven to 200°C/400°F/gas mark 6.

Peel and finely chop the onions, finely slice the carrots into rounds, deseed the red peppers and cut into thin strips, then put them all into a mixing bowl. Add the oil and salt, mix well, then spread the veg out on a baking tray. Roast in the oven for 20–25 minutes.

Remove the outer layer of skin from the head of garlic and chop the top off, leaving the tips of the cloves revealed. Place on a rack in the oven to bake at the same time as the veg.

In a large family-size pot, put the chopped tomatoes, harissa, cumin, coriander, smoked paprika, cinnamon, black pepper, stock, bay leaf, lemon juice, 1 teaspoon of the lemon zest and the honey/maple syrup/agave syrup. Turn the heat up high, bring to the boil, then reduce to a simmer.

Drain and rinse the chickpeas and add to the pot.

Once the veg and garlic are cooked, take them out of the oven. Squeeze the garlic cloves out of their skins (they should be really mushy and gooey), chop them roughly and add to the pot with the roasted veg. Check the seasoning and add salt and black pepper if required. Cook for a further 5 minutes.

Roughly chop the parsley and stir three-quarters of it into the soup. Garnish with the rest of the chopped parsley and lemon zest.

SERVES 4–6

2 onions
2 carrots
3 red peppers
2 tablespoons oil
1 teaspoon salt
1 head of garlic
2 x 400g tins of
    chopped tomatoes
2 tablespoons harissa paste
2 teaspoons ground cumin
2 teaspoons ground coriander
½ teaspoon smoked paprika
1 teaspoon ground cinnamon
½ teaspoon freshly ground
    black pepper
600ml vegetable stock or water
1 bay leaf
juice of 1 lemon
2 teaspoons lemon zest
1 tablespoon honey/maple syrup/
    agave syrup
2 x 400g tins of chickpeas
a large bunch of fresh
    flat-leaf parsley

VIETNAMESE PHO SOUP

A lovely noodle soup with a nourishing aromatic spiced broth and some meaty mushroom loveliness! This soup is best eaten straight away, as if left the noodles will swell.

Peel the garlic, ginger and onion and chop finely. Thinly slice the mushrooms. Cut the carrots in half lengthwise and slice into thin rounds. Finely chop the pak choi.

Pour the oil into a large pot and put on a high heat. Add the onion, garlic, ginger and mushrooms and fry for 5 minutes, stirring regularly.

Meanwhile, mix the tamari, sesame oil, lime juice and honey together in a cup. Add this mixture to the pot and cook for 3 minutes, until the mushrooms have absorbed the liquid.

Add the stock to the pot along with the carrots, cinnamon, star anise and cloves. Bring to the boil, then reduce to a simmer and cook for 15 minutes, stirring occasionally.

Five minutes before you want to serve the soup, add the noodles and leave to cook as per the packet instructions. Add the pak choi. While the noodles and pak choi are cooking, chop the scallions at an angle into thin slices. Once the noodles are cooked, divide them between 4 bowls, using a slotted spoon.

Now season the soup with salt and pepper if necessary, then divide it up so that each bowl is full. Add some beansprouts, scallions, pickled ginger and chilli to garnish, then cut the lime into quarters and put one quarter on the edge of each bowl.

SERVES 4–6

2 cloves of garlic
a thumb-size piece
  of fresh ginger
1 red onion
250g mushrooms
  (ideally shiitake or oyster)
4 carrots
1 medium pak choi
2 tablespoons oil
5 tablespoons tamari
2 tablespoons sesame oil
juice of 1 lime
1 tablespoon honey
2.5 litres vegetable stock
2 cinnamon sticks
2 star anise
3 whole cloves
4 nests of wholewheat
  noodles (200g)
salt and freshly ground
  black pepper

To garnish:
100g beansprouts
4 scallions
pickled ginger
1 chilli, sliced (if you like it hot)
1 lime

BEETROOT, COCONUT, GINGER AND LEMONGRASS SOUP

Our friend and chef John Donnelly first started cooking a version of this soup in the Happy Pear about eight years ago. It's a lovely sweet, creamy and earthy soup that's packed full of flavour. If you can't source fresh lemongrass, just use a little more fresh ginger instead and add the zest of half a lime.

Preheat the oven to 180°C/350°F/gas mark 4.

Peel and finely chop the onions. Wash the beetroot and scrub the skin, then chop, leaving the skin on. Peel the celeriac and chop into small pieces. Put the beetroot, onion, celeriac and the unpeeled cloves of garlic on a baking tray. Coat well with the oil, sprinkle with the salt, and bake for 25–30 minutes in the preheated oven until tender.

Peel and grate the ginger and bruise the lemongrass with the back of your knife to release its flavours. Tie the softened stalks into knots.

Put the coconut milk, vegetable stock, ginger, lemongrass, bay leaf and black pepper into a large family-size pot on a high heat. Bring to the boil, then reduce to a simmer, stirring well.

Once the veg in the oven are baked, add them to the pot, making sure to remove the garlic cloves from their skins before adding. Cover with a lid and cook gently for 15 minutes, stirring occasionally.

Remove the pot from the heat, take out the knotted lemongrass and the bay leaf, and blend the soup until smooth, using a stick blender. If it seems too thick, add a little water to reach the desired consistency. Taste, and season with more salt and pepper if needed.

Serve with a squeeze of lime in each bowl. You could also drizzle some coconut milk over and scatter with toasted pumpkin seeds.

SERVES 4–6

3 onions
600g uncooked beetroot
200g celeriac
5 cloves of garlic
2 tablespoons oil
2 teaspoons salt
½ a thumb-size piece of
  fresh ginger
2 stalks of fresh lemongrass
1 x 400ml tin of coconut milk
2 litres vegetable stock or water
1 bay leaf
½ teaspoon freshly ground
  black pepper
juice of 1 lime

SILKY WHITE SOUP: CELERIAC, PARSNIP AND CAULIFLOWER SOUP

Silky smooth white yumminess! This soup goes down particularly well when served with a big hunk of crusty bread.

Peel and finely slice the onion and garlic. Peel the celeriac and chop into bite-size pieces. Chop the parsnips into bite-size pieces. Cut the florets of cauliflower from the tough central stalk and finely chop them.

Put the oil in a large pot on a high heat. Add the onion and garlic and cook for 5 minutes, stirring regularly. Add the celeriac, parsnips, cauliflower and salt and give it all a good stir, then put the lid on the pot, reduce to a medium heat and leave to cook for 5 minutes, stirring occasionally. Remove the lid, add the white wine and leave to simmer on a reduced heat for further 5 minutes.

Drain and rinse the butterbeans and add them to the pot with the stock, black pepper and thyme leaves. Turn the heat up high and bring to the boil, then reduce to a simmer for a further 15 minutes. Remove from the heat and blend with a stick blender.

Garnish with a drizzle of green pesto, if using, and a light scattering of chilli flakes.

SERVES 4–6

1 onion
3 cloves of garlic
250g celeriac
2 parsnips
400g cauliflower
2 tablespoons oil
1 teaspoon salt
180ml white wine
1 x 400g tin of butterbeans
2.2 litres vegetable stock or water
½ teaspoon freshly ground black pepper
leaves from a few sprigs of fresh thyme
4–6 tablespoons green pesto, to garnish (optional)
chilli flakes, to garnish

FIVE-MINUTE MISO SOUP

A deeply nourishing and comforting soup that is great for a late evening supper or for when you don't have the energy to make a full meal. Or if you need a hangover cure! Use whatever type of dried seaweed you have or that is available (see page 259 for more on seaweed). Same goes for the miso paste – all types have a lovely, salty taste (see page 253 for more on miso).

First make your miso base. Peel the garlic and ginger, then chop the garlic and grate the ginger. In a blender, blend the warm water with the garlic, grated ginger and tamari.

Prepare your topping by slicing the scallion at an angle and slicing the chilli (seeds removed). Set aside.

Transfer your miso base into a medium-size pot on a medium heat and add the dried seaweed. If using any of the optional extras, add them now. Once the soup is hot enough (below boiling point), turn the heat off and stir the miso through with a fork.

Serve in bowls, with some scallions and red chilli sprinkled on top.

SERVES 2

2 cloves of garlic
½ a thumb-size piece of fresh ginger
1 litre warm water
3 tablespoons tamari/soy sauce
4 teaspoons dried seaweed, such as arame, or 1 strip of kombu
1½ tablespoons fresh miso

For the topping:
1 scallion
½ a red chilli

Optional extras to bulk it out:
½ a carrot, grated
4 tablespoons firm tofu (50g), chopped into small cubes
8 shiitake mushrooms
100g cooked noodles
2 tablepoons dried mushrooms

SIMPLE MUSHROOM AND LENTIL SOUP

There's something really hearty and deeply nourishing about a mushroom soup crossed with lentils – it's like a fireside on a damp day . . . guaranteed to warm you up from the inside out!

Peel and finely chop the garlic and onion. Finely slice the carrots into rounds, peel and chop the celeriac and cut the button mushrooms into quarters.

Put the oil into a large pot and place on a high heat. Add the onion and garlic and cook for about 5 minutes, stirring regularly. Add the carrots, celeriac, mushrooms and salt and cook, stirring regularly, for a further 5 minutes. Add the white wine and cook for a few minutes on a reduced heat.

Drain and rinse the lentils and add to the pot, together with the fresh thyme leaves and stock. Give it a good stir. Turn the heat up high and bring to the boil, then reduce the heat and simmer gently, uncovered, for 15 minutes.

Once cooked, remove from the heat and blend with a stick blender until smooth.

Finely slice the chives and use them to garnish each serving.

SERVES 4–6

3 cloves of garlic

1 onion

2 carrots

250g celeriac

350g button mushrooms

2 tablespoons oil

2 teaspoons salt

180ml white wine

2 x 400g tins of green or
    brown lentils

leaves from a small bunch
    of fresh thyme

2 litres vegetable stock

a small bunch of chives,
    to garnish

WATERCRESS AND ROASTED WALNUT SOUP

Watercress is mighty stuff, great for iron and for building your immune system. Instead of butter, cream and potatoes, we've gone for celeriac for body and roasted walnuts to give the soup a certain 'je ne sais quoi'. Lovely with a nice squeeze of lemon and some crumbled, roasted walnuts on top.

Peel the garlic and celeriac. Finely chop the garlic and cut the celeriac into small chunks. Finely slice the leeks, including the green tops.

Pour the oil into a large pot and put on a high heat. Add the garlic and fry for 1 minute, stirring occasionally. Add the leek and cook for 5 minutes, stirring regularly. Then add the celeriac and salt and stir. Turn down the heat, cover with a lid and leave to cook for a further 5 minutes.

Add the stock, bay leaf, leaves from the thyme sprigs and black pepper, then turn the heat up to high and bring to the boil. Once boiling, reduce the heat and simmer, still uncovered, for 10 minutes.

Add three-quarters of the walnuts and cook for 2 minutes. Remove from the heat and add the watercress, stirring to mix it right through.

Blend using a stick blender, leaving the mixture somewhat chunky, still with plenty of texture from the walnuts and watercress. Finish with a nice squeeze of lemon and garnish with the rest of the walnuts crumbled over the top.

SERVES 4

2 cloves of garlic
250g celeriac
2 leeks
2 tablespoons oil
2 teaspoons salt
2 litres vegetable stock or water
1 bay leaf
a few sprigs of fresh thyme
¼ teaspoon freshly ground
   black pepper
100g toasted walnuts
200g watercress
½ a lemon

OUR SECRET OF HAPPINESS – BEING PART OF SOMETHING BIGGER THAN OURSELVES!

We were very fortunate to grow up in a small place like Greystones, County Wicklow. Greystones is one of those towns where most people greet one another when they pass each other. It's a simple thing, but something we really miss when we go elsewhere. (Sometimes in London we have fun trying to engage people on the Tube. Most times we get ignored and people probably think we are just weird!)

Greystones is our own version of the Shire out of *The Hobbit* and *The Lord of the Rings* (the idyllic rural haven where hobbits like to grow things and simple things matter). We took this for granted until we went travelling 'in search of truth' in our early twenties. Among other things Dave went to an international Rainbow Gathering in Costa Rica. On paper this Rainbow Gathering was all about community and sharing and based on really lovely high ideals and values, so it was perfect for an impressionable twenty-two-year-old. People called one another 'brother' and 'sister' and it was the ultimate hippie gathering, all about the love! In reality Dave found it somewhat contrived and exclusive, and far removed from the genuine sense of community we always felt growing up in Greystones.

Feeling a part of something is a really basic human need and it goes deeper than how many 'friends' you have on Facebook or how perfect your life looks on Instagram. With the pace of modern life many people's experience of community can be largely online, when what we are really after is belonging to a group of people that is physically connected, whether that be family, friends, workmates, etc. Something as simple as a smile from a stranger can make someone's day better. We believe that feeling a sense of community is as important and nourishing as eating your greens!

Greystones is beside the sea and is a windy little town. People regularly suggest putting wind breakers – those barriers that cordon off an area – on the pavement around the tables at the front of our café. Steve is always really against these, as he wants the front of the café to be 'porous' and open and accessible to everyone passing. Steve is not really a barrier kind of guy!

In a way, that says a lot about our philosophy. We are open to everyone. For us community is completely inclusive and unpretentious, and right from the start we wanted to create a place that was universally accessible and not exclusive to a certain age group or type of person. We weren't all about creating a haven simply for the health nuts, but rather somewhere for absolutely everyone. In our first book we shared all the things we have done to build up our connections in the community. Among other things . . .

We have given away free porridge in the mornings for the past five years – we regard the warm and fuzzy feeling we get for doing something for free as the true profit!

We put on baking festivals at the drop of a hat (Apple Pie; Autumn Fruits; Chocolate; Brown Bread; Summer Fruits; Flapjack; Banana Bread). In one of our apple pie contests, as well as the usual band playing, we also had a hot tub out front for all to enjoy. There's nothing like having a bath with your friends on a Sunday afternoon while watching the cars go by on your main street!

Getting kids eating healthy is high up on our agenda. We have been involved in the local schools right since we started, usually doing demos during Healthy Eating Week and helping with raffle prizes, sponsoring school diaries, and generally trying to get kids on board with the message that fruit and veg can be cool too!

As a result of everything we do, our community has expanded far beyond our own family and friends – and it keeps expanding. We love it! Now people come to the HP maybe after reading our first book or watching a video to see for themselves what is going on and what our place is all about. Hopefully in the process we are helping to inspire them to be happier and healthier!

We asked some of our regulars what they think about being part of the Happy Pear community. We just want to show that, given the opportunity, people enjoy being part of something.

SHOP
·CAFE →
RESTAURANT →

SIOBHÁN

I am one of many who rocked up to the Happy Pear and offered to work for free. The café had just opened. The juice bar was a huge attraction with everyone waiting for their new-found elixir – many of them ladies hoping to catch a glimpse of the two handsome locals! They were shameless flirts and you could be forgiven for thinking that they fancied you, but they treated everyone the same, always smiling and saying a kind word. One day they had a problem with the dishwashing and I said, 'I will make your cutlery shine and I will do it for nothing.' (I already had a job elsewhere.) 'Brilliant, can you start tomorrow?' they said, and so it began.

I loved the Happy Pear and its chaotic ways. When I asked Dave who was going to replace a staff member who was leaving his reply was, 'I don't know. They haven't shown up yet.' This is how it worked because, amazingly, the right person would walk in! The staff did everything – painting, decorating, advising. I worked with the bakers at night and helped produce the wonderful cakes. We also made the pesto – a far cry from today, when it's made by an entire team. There was no segregation between management and staff – we all worked, laughed, sang and partied with each other. We were all learning together and I loved the boys' ethos and drive.

The Happy Pear soon became the hub of the village. Eventually I quit my other job and went on the payroll. Over the years I have watched the business grow into what it is today. I am so happy to have been a part of it. Working in the Happy Pear is not just a job – it's an education and a way of life.

DENIS GRAY

Denis Gray is in most days for coffee and a scone. Denis is eighty-six and is a retired sea captain. He is an absolute legend and must have been a colossus in his prime (not unlike John Wayne!). He still swims in the sea twice daily and does spinning classes. Since his wife died a few years ago he has tried online dating and can still charm the ladies!

He pays little attention to common parking etiquette or rules of queuing in pursuit of his daily scone and Americano. We think that's fair enough at eighty-six – we love you, Denis! Denis has been part of the daily life for us for a good few years now, and at this stage we expect to see him just about every day. No matter the weather, he insists on sitting outside on the 'terrace', rain, sun or sleet.

Denis is a total inspiration, and if you ever feel like you're a bit stuck or bogged down in the small daily worries, taking one look at Denis reminds you of what matters. He is the embodiment of what we want to be when we grow old.

'The Happy Pear is not just the food, it's about the whole ambience: the general air of goodwill and a feel-good atmosphere that is very welcoming. If I'm on my own, it's a pleasant place to be. It's the sort of a place you would never feel lonely.'

PAUL BYRNE

Paul Byrne started the monthly film club in the HP. He works as a film critic and therefore is the perfect man to run a film club. He also runs the online Greystones Guide and is a wonderful asset to Greystones.

'There's no denying this cute little café has had a big effect on this cute little town. On any given sunny afternoon, you'll find plenty of people making the five-mile pilgrimage around Bray Head to Greystones, all heading to the Happy Pear to get their just desserts. Most likely with an organic, free-range, gluten-free cherry on top.

'If not quite certifiably a cult, the Happy Pear does go one step further than promoting a healthier lifestyle: these guys are offering a healthier way of life, inside and out. The Flynn twins are just as concerned with metaphysics as they are with mushroom broccoli roast, with mind-bending philosophies as they are with tongue-melting falafels. How else to explain the great big melting-pot of people who gather there day after day, some of them religiously, some of them cautiously, and most of them simply because they're bloody hungry?'

MICHAEL AND MEL

Michael and Mel both live just down the road from the HP. They write and illustrate children's books. As writers it's easy for them to live a bit in their own world, and they might not notice that they have barely left the house in a week, so the Happy Pear has become a way for them to stay connected with other people. Michael is from the States, and not having a network here it was easy for him to meet people and make friends.

Mel has written two novels and one picture book upstairs in the Happy Pear while drinking one-shot cappuccinos, and Michael has worked on about five picture books, drinking mostly lattes and munching on seeded cookies.

The Happy Pear is a part of their routine and some-where they can meet people. It's not too dissimilar to a modern version of the pub. They have noticed how the Happy Pear has helped Greystones become a healthy destination community for many to visit, eat some nice food, skim some stones on the water and get the train back to Dublin!

'When we started we didn't know how a kitchen worked or how to cook for loads of people. We gave Dorene a blank canvas to do her thing, and she took the ball and ran with it. She is one of the catalysts behind our food.'

DORENE AKA 'LADY P'

Dorene has been with us from Day One, when we had no idea of what we were doing. Dorene on the other hand had been cheffing the food we loved for more than twenty years, so took to what we wanted to do like a duck to water. She is an amazing woman and chef and at this stage a dear friend. She is one of those people that are ageless, as she can relate to people of all ages.

Dorene has a great veggie heritage. Her grand-aunt Olive Palmer opened a veggie café on Dublin's Westland Row around 1916. At that time there was a whole wave of veggie happenings in Britain and Ireland. The world-famous playwright George Bernard Shaw was one of the many eminent people who were veggie, including Dorene's granddad Avery and grand-aunt. In the next generation, all Dorene's aunts and uncles were veggie. Her uncle Alan had a veggie restaurant, the Vegetarian Café, in London in the 1960s where Dorene's mother worked when she was pregnant with Dorene.

When we started we didn't know how a kitchen worked or how to cook for loads of people. We gave Dorene a blank canvas to do her thing, and she took the ball and ran with it. She is one of the catalysts behind our food.

We love you, Dorene!

LARRY AND MONICA

Larry and Monica moved from Dublin to Greystones a few years back because they wanted a change to a healthier lifestyle. Part of the attraction was the Happy Pear – not just the healthy food, but just as important was the atmosphere of inclusion and sense of community. Larry has since moved away from his steak and chips diet to eating all things vegetable and feeling mighty!

'It's not a commune, but a community that you feel part of, and not in an anonymous coffee shop way,' says Larry. 'People chat to you as a human rather than a customer and it's a bit like dropping into someone's living room!'

'The Happy Pear team is a melting pot of like-minded people from all over the world coming together to have fun and try to make the earth a better place!'

The Happy Pear team is a melting pot of like-minded people from all over the world coming together to have fun and try to make the earth a better place! The members of our team really are our friends and extended family and we work really hard to make the place great to work in and to foster a team spirit.

Everyone has hobbies or interests outside of work and we encourage our team to share their passions, as these can often be incorporated into work. For instance, back in the early days when we had a juice bar, Aisling Leonard worked with us. Since being a world-class juicer in the HP she has travelled the world and trained as a yoga teacher. In 2014 we teamed up with her and now we offer free yoga classes twice weekly for staff.

Something not to be underestimated is the bonding power of a party. Raj is an amazing human who works with us; he has a massive appetite for life and just like a puppy he is bursting with energy, fun and enthusiasm. He is our head of HP parties and he organizes a get-together every couple of months. The first ever Happy Pear party was a cross-dressing fancy-dress Halloween party! Often times we have had our Christmas party in March. There's nothing better than everyone dancing together to foster team spirit!

We now have a team of about eighty people working with us, so keeping them up to date with what is going on can be pretty challenging. Last year, Sarah, who does PR and Marketing, started writing a Pear's Weekly Digest, which is an amusing weekly two-pager on some of the fun stuff happening across all the bits of the Happy Pear (from pesto kitchen, to farm, to baking, to coffee department, to shop, to restaurant, to office). Each week a team within our team is featured and has to write something funny about what they do, so that the wider team can see who is involved and what they are up to.

RUAIDHRI

CATHY

JENNIFER

RAJ

SHANE

DENIS NOONAN

GONG PING

JACK

DONNCHA

DARRAGH

JUAN

PAUL

YURI

NAOMI D.

AUSSIE PAUL

NAOMI S.

DANICA AND KEN MURPHY

Danica and Ken live directly across the road from our shop and café in Greystones. They sleep at the front of their house with their window slightly ajar. On weekend mornings they hear us setting up. From the speakers outside, and even without looking out, they can tell the weather from the music we're playing!

'If it's a cloudy day the tunes tend to be mellow – it's Bob Marley drifting through the open window,' says Danica. 'Warmer days and there's a higher-energy house vibe. Then we hear the clicks and scrapes of tables and chairs being put into position.

'All day and long into the evenings, we see the people coming and going from the Happy Pear: cyclists; day hikers; dog walkers; mums with prams and strollers; pensioners out for the day on their travel pass; foreign visitors attracted by the steady hum of activity; loyal locals looking for a friendly hello as they shop for fruit and veg, or stop for a pick-me-up cuppa tea or coffee and some fabulous treat; vegetarians in search of culinary inspiration; people treating themselves to dinner out; and neighbours like us who consider the Happy Pear an extension of our kitchen.

'To us, the Happy Pear is the modern healthy food/coffee culture version of the television sitcom bar Cheers. It's where everyone knows your name, there is always a chat to be had, and you just never know what the guys will get up to next!'

ANTO

Anto is the modern-day Renaissance man who is good at loads of things, from carpentry to body-building to cheffing. And he can also do back-flips! He built our 'prison gym' that we use down at the back of the shop! He was the catalyst that brought lots of the team together to do four-minute Tabata workouts, to break up our working day.

Anto is also a great man for the outdoors and exploring the Wicklow hills. He started the Happy Pear hikers last year and leads the group around his favourite Wicklow hikes most weeks in summer. It's a great way of coming together, having a good laugh outdoors, and exploring the wilds of where we live. This started out as a staff thing, but after posting some of the photos of the cool spots he brings us to on social media, others outside of the Happy Pear team have started coming along.

MICHAEL AND JOE

Michael and Joe, identical twins, arrived on 20 March 2007 as sixteen-year-olds doing work experience. They're now twenty-five and are still working with us. They have paid their way through school, college and several international adventures largely by washing dishes in the Happy Pear!

Michael claims to have washed half a million cups and believes he could claim squatters' rights in the washroom by now! They have grown up while being part of the Happy Pear journey and seen it evolve from a place that only locals came to, to one now where people are coming from all over to see what is going on.

OUR ONLINE COMMUNITY

Our online community has really helped us expand our tribe of like-minded people all over the world.

However, much as we love social media we know it is not the be-all and end-all when it comes to community. It makes it all worthwhile when social media comes to life in the form of real people who say that we have touched their lives in some small way. We find it amazing when someone who we know from Twitter or Instagram pops into the Happy Pear to say hello. It makes us realize that our online following is a living breathing community full of real people with ideas and feelings! For instance, recently a lovely Irish guy who lives in Bermuda popped in. He was home for a visit and just wanted to say hi and see our set-up after following us on social media for some time.

In 2014 we became part of Jamie Oliver's Food-Tube Network. We regularly shoot videos for his channel and sometimes write for his website. In doing so we have also become part of one of the largest food communities in Europe. As part of this we go to London for filming and to do events. It's really amazing when someone in the UK comes up and says they love what we do and really feels they have a connection with us from social media! And going to London regularly is really fun and is a nice contrast to our Shire-like existence in Greystones!

SALADS

CARAMELIZED FIG SALAD WITH BAKED SWEET POTATO AND WALNUTS

Fresh figs are one of Steve's favourite fruits, so he had a ball coming up with a salad that celebrated both the fresh and the dried fig along with sweet potatoes, greens and walnuts to bring the whole salad to life!

Preheat the oven to 180°C/350°F/gas mark 4.

Chop the dried figs into small pieces and remove the hard bits where the fig joined the tree. Soak the figs in the balsamic vinegar and water for 5 minutes, making sure they are all submerged.

Clean and scrub the sweet potatoes, removing any dirt. Leaving the skin on, cut them into chunky wedges and put them on a baking tray, coating them with the oil and ½ teaspoon of salt. Bake in the preheated oven for 20 minutes, until lovely and soft and starting to crisp around the edges.

While the sweet potatoes are baking, cut the fresh figs into thick slices.

Drain the dried figs, reserving the liquid. Pour the liquid into a frying pan and add the honey/maple syrup and the remaining ½ teaspoon of salt. Put the heat on high, place the fresh figs in the pan and keep the liquid moving until it starts to reduce and become a syrup. This will get the fresh figs caramelized and infused with a sweet balsamic flavour. Once this liquid is syrupy, turn the heat off. Don't move the frying pan much, as you want to keep the fresh figs intact.

Get a large salad bowl and put the washed rocket in the bottom, keeping a few leaves for the top. Add the baked sweet potatoes and the dried and caramelized figs. Pour the syrup over the top. Scatter the remaining rocket leaves over, then sprinkle with the walnuts, crushed lightly with your hands.

SERVES 4

60g dried figs
6 tablespoons balsamic vinegar
10 tablespoons water
2 sweet potatoes
2 tablespoons oil
1 teaspoon sea salt
4 fresh figs
3 tablespoons honey/
    maple syrup
100g rocket/green salad leaves
50g walnuts

BEETROOT SALAD

Our handsome Brazilian chefs dreamed up this salad. They never ate beetroot in Brazil and now they want to put it in all their salads! This is easy to make, sweet, crunchy and rocking.

Remove the dirt from the beetroot, top and tail, then scrub the skin, but don't peel. Grate the beetroot into a large bowl, add the salt and leave to sit for a few minutes. Put the frozen peas into a bowl of warm water and leave to thaw.

Toast the pumpkin seeds in a dry frying pan for a few minutes until they start to pop, then set aside.

Put the yoghurt into a bowl with the tahini and honey. Chop the mint leaves very finely, add to the bowl and mix well. Mix the yoghurt-tahini dressing with the beetroot until it all goes wonderfully pink!

Add the peas and the pumpkin seeds just before you're ready to serve, otherwise the peas will turn pink and the seeds will go soft.

SERVES 6, AS A SIDE

500g uncooked beetroot
1 teaspoon sea salt
250g frozen peas
100g pumpkin seeds
250g natural yoghurt
3 tablespoons tahini
2 tablespoons honey
20g fresh mint leaves

TWO-MINUTE 'ROCK-ET STAR' SALAD

A great friend of ours is a musician and makes this salad before going on stage, as he can get the ingredients in most parts of world. It looks great, and is healthy, tasty and easy to make when on the move!

Wash the rocket and the berries. Get a bowl and put the rocket in.

Cut the avocado in half, then remove the stone and cut each half into small pieces, still in the skin, making sure not to cut through. Spoon out the flesh and add to the bowl of rocket.

Squeeze in the lemon juice, using your hand as a sieve to catch any pips, and add a pinch of salt. Mix through.

If you're making this salad at home and have some olive oil handy, mix it in to make it even better!

Once the salad is dressed, add the seeds/nuts and finally top with the berries.

SERVES 4, AS A SIDE

80–100g rocket, or similar green
   salad leaf
125g raspberries
125g blueberries
1 ripe avocado
juice of ½ a lemon
a pinch of salt
2 tablespoons olive oil (optional)
a handful of pumpkin seeds/
   walnuts/nuts of your choice

FENNEL, RUBY GRAPEFRUIT, AVOCADO AND BLUEBERRY SALAD

This is a lovely light and fresh salad – crunchy fennel, creamy avocado, sharp, sweet grapefruit, juicy blueberries and mint giving a burst of summer flavour!

Wash the fennel and chop it into super-thin small strips about 5cm long, making sure you remove any larger pieces and chopping them up finely. You want to ensure they are really fine, as they are the base of the salad and you want them to feel light and fresh. Transfer to a large bowl, add ½ teaspoon of salt, and mix really well – the salt will help to soften the fennel.

Peel the grapefruit, using a knife so you remove the bitter pith – the thin white layer between the skin and the flesh. Cut the segments out of the membrane between them. Add the grapefruit segments to the bowl of fennel.

Cut the avocados in half, remove their stones and cut each half into small pieces still in the skin, making sure not to cut through. Scrape these pieces off the skin and add to the bowl. Mix with the fennel and grapefruit until the avocado pieces break down and begin to act like a creamy dressing.

Finely chop the mint and mix it through, then top with the blueberries.

SERVES 4–6, AS A SIDE

2 fennel bulbs (approx. 400g)
½ teaspoon sea salt
2 large ruby grapefruit
2 ripe avocados
25g fresh mint
125g blueberries

COURGETTE RIBBONS WITH POMEGRANATE AND WALNUT

This juicy, fresh, simple to make salad has a distinctive Middle Eastern flavour. If you can't find pomegranate molasses, you could replace with more honey and a tiny splash of lime juice. This salad has to be eaten fresh, as if left to sit it becomes soggy.

Cut the courgettes in half. Using a potato peeler, make long courgette 'ribbons', dropping them into a bowl.

In a cup, mix together the tahini, pomegranate molasses and honey/maple syrup/agave syrup and pour over the courgette ribbons, making sure the liquid from the courgettes mixes with the tahini to form a uniform dressing.

Cut the pomegranate in half. Put one half face down on a chopping board and bang the back with a wooden spoon until the seeds fall out. Repeat with the other half. Now rinse the seeds, removing any white pith and juice (you don't want the juice, as it will make the sauce too runny and will dye the courgettes red).

Toast the walnuts in a dry frying pan, turning regularly until they start to brown. Put in the centre of a clean dry tea towel and bring the four corners together. Hold firmly and bang on a table to crush the walnuts – more fun than using a knife!

Mix most of the crushed walnuts and pomegranate seeds with the courgettes, reserving a few to sprinkle over the top before serving.

SERVES 4

2 courgettes
(1 green and 1 yellow)
1½ tablespoons tahini
(or use peanut butter)
1 tablespoon pomegranate molasses
1 teaspoon honey/maple syrup/ agave syrup
1 pomegranate
100g walnuts

MEDITERRANEAN GRILLED VEG SALAD
WITH CHARRED HALLOUMI

Charred, sweet grilled summer veg with strips of halloumi, topped off with a tahini yoghurt dressing – this gorgeous salad will leave everyone looking for more! Great served with a couple of slices of nice bread.

Preheat the oven to 200°C/400°F/gas mark 6.

Slice the aubergine, courgette and carrots lengthwise into ½cm strips. Deseed the peppers and cut them into big chunks. Cut the red onion in half, remove its outer skin and separate off the layers so each will get nicely baked. Cut the rough ends off the asparagus.

Put all the vegetables into a large bowl and mix with the oil and salt.

Lay the aubergines, courgettes, carrots, peppers, and onions on two large baking trays and put into the oven for 15–20 minutes, until the veggies are starting to char and become tender.

About halfway through the cooking time, slice the halloumi into 3 decent rectangles. Lay them on a separate baking tray with the asparagus and put into the oven with the veggies, until the halloumi is starting to turn golden and the asparagus spears are tender. The halloumi and asparagus will take about 8 minutes – keep an eye on the veggies and take them out when they are ready.

Mix the ingredients for the dressing in a small bowl.

Layer up three plates evenly with the grilled veggies and top with the asparagus spears and halloumi. Serve the dressing on the side.

SERVES 3 (GENEROUSLY)

1 aubergine
1 courgette
2 carrots
2 red peppers
1 red onion
200g asparagus
4 tablespoons olive oil
1 teaspoon sea salt
1 x 200g block of halloumi cheese

For the dressing
100ml natural yoghurt
2 tablespoons olive oil
2 teaspoons tahini
1 teaspoon sea salt
juice of 1 lime

LENTILS WITH GOAT'S CHEESE AND ROASTED PUMPKIN SALAD

One of Dave's top five favourite veg is the pumpkin – he even won a local competition for one of his home-grown ones! If you can get a kabocha squash (green with yellow flesh) or an orange Hokkaido pumpkin these are fab, but just use a peeled butternut squash if you can't.

Preheat the oven to 180°C/350°F/gas mark 4.

Cut the pumpkin in half and remove the seeds. Leaving its skin on, chop the pumpkin into wedges and put on to a baking tray. Sprinkle with 2 tablespoons of oil and 1 teaspoon of salt and mix, coating the pumpkin wedges evenly. Bake in the preheated oven for 30–40 minutes, until they start to brown and become tender and caramelized.

Peel and finely slice your onion and garlic. Deseed the red pepper and chop into bite-size pieces. Slice the courgette into rounds and chop the mushrooms into quarters.

Pour 2 tablespoons of oil into a medium-size pot and put on a high heat. Add the onions and garlic and cook for 5 minutes, stirring regularly. Add the courgettes, red pepper, mushrooms, 2 teaspoons of salt and the black pepper, and cook for another 5 minutes, stirring regularly.

Add the lentils, stock, thyme leaves, bay leaf, paprika and tamari and give it all a good mix. Bring to the boil, then reduce the heat to a simmer and cook until all the liquid has been absorbed. The lentils should be soft and tender and still moist, not dried out – if they are, add a little more liquid and cook until they are ready.

Put half the rocket leaves into a large salad bowl, spreading them right around the edges of the bowl. Pour the hot lentil mix into the centre of the bowl.

Top with the baked pumpkin wedges and the rest of the rocket leaves and sprinkle over the goat's cheese/feta cheese. Give a little mix before serving.

Lovely eaten warm or cold.

SERVES 4–6

1kg pumpkin or squash
4 tablespoons oil
3 teaspoons salt
1 red onion
3 cloves of garlic
1 red pepper
1 courgette
150g button mushrooms
½ teaspoon freshly ground
    black pepper
250g green/brown/speckled
    blue dried lentils
1 litre vegetable stock
leaves from a few sprigs
    of fresh thyme
1 bay leaf
2 teaspoons paprika
3 tablespoons tamari/soy sauce
200g rocket leaves
200g crumbly goat's cheese/
    feta cheese

MELLEN'S BONE-BUILDING SALAD

Our dear friend and colleague Mellen is really into strong healthy bones: she suffers from osteopenia (a condition that affects bone health) and is always looking for food to build the strength of her bones. Her salad is full of things that are rich in calcium and high in minerals that help your body to absorb calcium. Mel says that if you added a boiled egg to the mix you'd increase the bone protection factor even more. Not only is Mellen's salad good for you, but it's also really delicious!

Rinse the rocket and cut into bite-size pieces. Halve the cherry tomatoes. Put all these into a salad bowl.

Cut the avocado in half, remove the stone and score through the flesh in each half, up and down and then across, making sure not to cut through the skin. Then scrape these pieces into the bowl.

Rinse the alfalfa sprouts well and drain in a colander so not too much water is left on them. Add to the bowl with the flaked almonds and sesame seeds.

Finely chop the garlic, then mix all the dressing ingredients in a mug and pour over the salad.

Toss well and enjoy!

SERVES 2

100g fresh rocket
6–8 cherry tomatoes
1 ripe avocado
1 x 80g punnet of alfalfa sprouts
50g toasted almond flakes
1 heaped tablespoon of toasted
   sesame seeds

For the dressing:
1 clove of garlic
juice of ½ a lemon
a drizzle of very good cold-
   pressed virgin olive oil
a pinch of unrefined sea salt or
   Himalayan salt

THREE-COLOUR QUINOA PROTEIN SALAD

This salad looks and tastes amazing, and with each mouthful you just know it is doing you a world of good! Great if you have a gang coming over. Once assembled, it will keep, undressed, for a couple of days in the fridge.

Cook the quinoa according to the instructions on page 255. Once cooked, put into a large mixing bowl and leave to cool for 15 minutes.

Thaw the frozen peas/edamame beans in warm water for 5–10 minutes.

On a chopping board, cut off the tops and bottoms of the oranges and peel them, removing all the white pith. Individually cut out each segment, slicing along both sides of the membrane to release the segment on to your knife. Place the segments in a bowl, and squeeze out the juice of what is left of the orange too.

Slice the radicchio in half, then cut out and discard the hard triangular core at the end of each half and finely slice the leaves.

Finely chop the mint leaves. Toast the cashews in a dry frying pan for a few minutes.

Mix all the dressing ingredients together.

Drain and rinse the peas/edamame beans, ensuring they are at room temperature. Once the quinoa has cooled, add the radicchio, cashews, goji berries, mint and peas/edamame beans.

Dress as much of the salad as you are going to use, top with the orange segments, and serve.

SERVES 6–8

250g three-colour quinoa
160g frozen peas/
    edamame beans
4 small oranges
1 head of radicchio
leaves from 5 sprigs of fresh mint
80g cashew nuts
5 tablespoons goji berries

For the dressing:
juice of 2 limes
1 tablespoon honey/agave syrup
1 tablespoon balsamic vinegar
4 tablespoons olive oil
½ teaspoon sea salt
pinch of freshly ground
    black pepper

EVERYBODY CAN BE HEALTHY!

In our experience there is no perfect diet. It is not like: eat five stalks of kale, a head of broccoli, a green juice and some spirulina every day and you'll live till 150. Throw in some fresh turmeric and chia seeds you'll make it to 160! We are not machines, and we have unique genetic make-ups and individual personalities and emotions and thankfully we are all different. Still, the general message to EAT MORE VEG is a hard one to contest.

Health is not just about the absence of disease or about living longer or having lower cholesterol. It's also about feeling good, having enough energy to really enjoy yourself, being happy in your body, being able to move and feel good about yourself.

According to the World Health Organization (WHO), if people in Ireland and the UK do not change their habits to a healthier lifestyle we'll all be facing an obesity crisis. This does not need to happen, and if we are open to new habits we can help make things better.

Health is, as the cliché goes, not so much a destination as a journey. It is something to work at – being aware, cultivating good habits, trying to stop bad ones developing. In most cases, heart disease, Type 2 diabetes and obesity can be radically improved or reversed by adopting a plant-based whole-food diet and lifestyle.

As a species we are hard-wired to crave fat and sugar. The Happy Pear kids are no different from yours. Steve's May (5) and Theo (2) would both happily sell their souls for a handful of jellies. A few years back Steve caught May on the floor beside the fridge having devoured a quarter pound of butter straight from the pack!

May was just behaving like a normal mammal – seeking out high-calorie food to help her survive. That's what we mammals are programmed to do. For millennia that made sense, because humans didn't know where their next meal was coming from and how hard they would have to work to get it. Nowadays we can walk into shops and buy processed foods with varying degrees of sugar, fat, salt, all packed with calories. Because there is almost no fibre in processed foods, we absorb these calories with little effort and often get a buzz after eating them, signalling 'Well done you, on finding all those calories!' This is a pleasure trap that can trick us into thinking that processed foods are more desirable than whole foods. In contrast, low-calorie high-fibre natural foods – a baked potato, say – do not deliver quite the same hit but are much better for us in the long run.

We all have the potential to be healthy, fit and lean. Indeed, we believe that each of us should be able to live long disease-free lives. It takes a little more thought and effort to adopt a more plant-based diet, but it is our passion and our mission to demonstrate that it's possible to eat absolutely delicious food that's also good for you.

CALCIUM COMES FROM PLANTS!

One of the hardest things for people to accept on our healthy eating courses is that they can get enough calcium without dairy. When we were young, every day we got six litres of milk delivered to our door and drank a litre each, all six of us. We absolutely loved the stuff! So we completely understand people's attachment to cow's milk. And we also understand why people get a little heated when we suggest that while cow's milk is the perfect food for a calf to grow approximately 200kg in six months, humans are not calves!

We are one of the few species to consume the breast milk of another species. We are also one of the few mammals to consume milk after weaning. Calcium is for strong bones, so you would imagine mammals with massive frames need a whole lot of calcium. Yet we don't see elephants, giraffes, rhinos or gorillas searching for a lactating cow (or indeed a lactating female of their own species) to get their recommended daily amount (RDA) of calcium!

Calcium is a mineral. It is found in the soil, where it is absorbed into the roots of plants. The highest sources of easily absorbable calcium are plant foods such as dark green leafy vegetables. This is where all those animals get their calcium – from eating their roots and greens. Seeds, particularly sesame, are also an excellent source.

This may surprise you: countries with the highest rates of dairy consumption per capita – the USA, New Zealand, Britain and Sweden – have the highest rates of the degenerative bone disease osteoporosis.

Also, those countries that consume the lowest levels of dairy products have the lowest levels of osteoporosis. And in recent studies vegans had higher bone mineral densities than omnivores, despite taking in lower levels of calcuim and protien. Their systems simply use what's available more effectively.

Many factors contribute to calcium loss, from age (older people lose more calcium) to a shortage of vitamin D, to excessive consumption of sodium (salt), protein and caffeine. The more of these three you take in, the more calcium you flush out. In stark contrast, most leafy green vegetables provide lots of easily absorbed calcium without causing calcium loss.

The single best thing you can do to prevent osteoporosis is to exercise, as the primary cause of osteoporosis is not simply a lack of calcium but also a lack of weight-bearing activity (e.g. walking, running, yoga). Weight-bearing activity strains the bones, the cells in the bones call out for more calcium and the calcium is absorbed.

GUESS WHAT? PROTEIN COMES FROM PLANTS TOO!

The most consistent question people ask us is, 'Where do you get your protein?' It's typically asked by young men or mothers of teenage boys. Just as with calcium, many people believe that meat is the only source of dietary protein. Challenging this is nothing short of heresy! Yet for the past fourteen years we have eaten nothing with a face or a mother – no meat, fish, dairy or eggs – and we feel we are getting all the protein we need.

Proteins consist of twenty different amino acids, eleven of which are made by our bodies. The remaining nine – the essential amino acids – we need to get from our diet. Protein is used primarily for growth and repair. The biggest growth spurt during our entire life cycle is during infancy: a baby literally doubles its weight in a matter of months. Since the most natural food for a baby is its mother's milk, it follows that breast milk must be very high in protein, mustn't it? Actually, no – breast milk contains about 5–6 per cent protein. The average western diet consists of about 15–30 per cent protein. And again looking at the animal kingdom, some of the biggest, fiercest animals in the world – the elephant, rhino, and gorilla – are plant-eating herbivores and they don't worry about where they get their protein.

Between them, the WHO and the FDA (America's Food and Drug Administration) say that humans need to have just 5–10 per cent of their calories coming from protein. Most plant foods deliver far more than this. In another US government study, this time of protein sources in various types of diet, the whole-food sample (i.e. plant foods) provided over 23 per cent protein – well beyond government guidelines. Other studies of vegetarians and vegans have shown that on average they get 70 per cent more protein than they need every day. Dr T. Colin Campbell, author of the global best-seller The China Study, tried to come up with a whole-food plant-based diet that did not contain adequate protein but found it virtually impossible.

Kevin Thornton is an Irish and European Triathlon champion who has been eating a totally plant-based diet for two years now. In fact, since going vegetarian Kevin has been feeling and performing better than ever. Which just goes to show that if an elite athlete can get everything he needs eating a plant-based diet, the rest of us can too! We are very proud to sponsor Kevin.

MOVE MORE AND STRESS LESS!

Although we seem to focus largely on food, and this book is about eating, we believe there are two other vital aspects of being healthy: getting enough exercise and managing stress.

Humans may have big brains and smart-phones, but we are mammals nonetheless and mammals need to move. We were fortunate. From the moment we could walk and run, our mom, the great Ismay Flynn (we love you, Mom!), had us out playing every sport she could find. We never looked back.

If a day goes by that we don't exercise, we really miss it and can get pent up, a bit like a dog that hasn't had its walk! We do our best to exercise every day – whether it be a dip in the sea, a ten-minute play around on the gym down the back of the shop, some yoga, a quick run, or even a few handstands. But you don't have to do handstands! We aren't even talking about running a 5km or joining a gym or a triathlon club. It doesn't have to be 'no pain, no gain' type stuff, but simple regular things like walking that everyone can do. Ideally try to get thirty minutes' exercise a day, or forty-five minutes five days a week. If you have had a busy day, even fifteen minutes is beneficial. Walking is an easy one. It's easy, cheap and gets you outdoors, which can do wonders for your mental state.

Think of times when you feel too tired to move and someone drags you out for a walk. You almost always feel better afterwards and are grateful. So exercise actually gives you energy and it's amazing for shifting staleness, clearing the head and rebooting. Last but not least, the best incentive to exercise is that it releases endorphins in your brain – just like the endorphins released during sex – making you feel fantastic!

The best time to exercise is whenever you can – whenever it fits into your day. Many people find exercising in the morning easier, as fewer things 'pop up' and get in the way. Introduce movement into your day: park one stop away from the train station or further away from the shops, and take the stairs instead of the lift. All the small things add up. Just get moving!

Just like wanting to stuff ourselves with high-energy foods, feeling stressed is totally natural. In situations where our survival is threatened – say being chased by a bear – our body produces adrenalin, our 'fight or flight' hormone. This increases our breathing, which in turn increases the amount of oxygen in our blood, giving us heightened alertness. At the same time all the systems not needed during this emergency situation (e.g. reproduction and digestion) shut down. The body's sole focus is escaping danger and surviving. Once we're safe, the adrenalin supply switches off and everything is restored to normal.

The thing is that our primitive bodies don't differentiate between being chased by a bear or a bank manager. As far as our systems are concerned, whatever is worrying us – the mortgage, ill health in the family, work pressures – is an imminent threat and everything goes on red alert. Because of modern life many of us are stressed for sustained periods of time, so important systems in our bodies shut down and don't perform as they should. All of this leads to illness, premature ageing and disease.

Some people thrive on stress and they don't seem to get sick. These are people who can turn it off, normally when they sleep. That's one of the keys to managing chronic stress – being able to turn it off. Most stress is based on worries about what might happen in the future. When you remain in the moment you are breaking that cycle of worry. Meditation, mindfulness and yoga are often suggested as ways of being in the moment. But whatever you like to do that absorbs you – gardening, darts, singing in a choir, swimming in the sea, taking a long bath, going to Mass – do more of it! Do what-ever gives you a sense of peace, relaxation and ease.

Here are some other tips for managing stress:

BREATHE.

When you become aware that you're feeling stressed, take some slow deep breaths. That will immediately reduce your stress levels.

CHECK YOUR POSTURE.

Are your shoulders, neck and back tight, clenched and raised? If so, take some deep breaths and try to soften your posture.

CONNECT.

It's easy to feel alone when you are stressed, and that can lead to a sense of isolation, depression and ill-health. But you are not on your own. Developing a sense of community is an antidote to the pressures of life. Reaching out to other people (even getting a pet) will give you perspective and a vital sense of connection to the wider world. Call a friend. Volunteer. Find a therapist. Talk to your mum or dad. Forgive. Make love with your partner. Go to church. Have dinner with your family . . . You get the idea.

'We often do four-minute Tabata workouts in our 'prison gym' at the back of the café. It's amazing breaking up the day; we all feel better, it boosts morale, and we always have a laugh.'

MAINS

MOROCCAN TAGINE

This great recipe is a quick and easy midweek dinner option. It's low in fat, bursting with vitamins, minerals and antioxidants, and once you've set up your store cupboard and don't have to buy everything for the recipe, it works out very good value for money. Great served with brown rice, flatbreads or toasted pitta bread, and wedges of lime or lemon.

Chop the aubergine into small bite-size pieces. Peel and finely chop the garlic and the onion. Deseed and chop the peppers and finely slice the carrots. Mix the water with the tamari/soy sauce.

Put the tamari mix into a large pot along with the aubergine, garlic, onion and paprika. Cook on a medium heat for 10 minutes, stirring regularly, until the aubergines are nicely softened.

Add the peppers and carrots to the pan along with the salt and black pepper, cumin, smoked paprika, cinnamon, ground ginger, the pinch of cayenne pepper/chilli powder and lemon juice. Stir everything well and cook for another 5 minutes.

Finely chop the dates and drain and rinse the chickpeas. Add the dates to the pan along with the chickpeas, chopped tomatoes and agave syrup/honey and mix well. Bring to the boil, then reduce the heat and cook for a further 15–20 minutes, until the carrots are cooked through.

Chop the fresh herbs and garnish each serving with these. If you like, top with almonds, harissa and slices of avocado and serve with wedges of lime.

SERVES 6–8

1 large aubergine
4 cloves of garlic
1 red onion
1 red pepper
1 yellow pepper
2 carrots
7 tablespoons water
5 tablespoons tamari/soy sauce
1 teaspoon paprika
1 teaspoon salt
½ teaspoon freshly ground
   black pepper
2 teaspoons ground cumin
1 teaspoon smoked paprika
2 teaspoons ground cinnamon
1 teaspoon ground ginger
a pinch of cayenne pepper/
   chilli powder
juice of ½ a lemon
8 pitted dates
1 x 400g tin of chickpeas
2 x 400g tins of good-quality
   chopped tomatoes
1 tablespoon agave syrup/ honey
a bunch of fresh flat-leaf parsley/
   coriander/chives
lime wedges, to serve

Optional toppings:
flaked almonds
harissa (see page 182)
avocado

MEXICAN SALSA, MIXED BEANS AND CORIANDER

This is a really quick easy dinner that has great depth of flavour and is full of aromatic flavours. It's great for midweek. It keeps for three days in the fridge, freezes well and is great for lunch the next day too! We nearly always serve this with brown rice for a hearty meal.

Peel the onion and garlic and chop them finely. Deseed the red pepper and the chilli, then cut the pepper into bite-size pieces and finely chop the chilli (include the seeds if you like it hot).

Put the onion and garlic into a large saucepan with the water and cook on a high heat for 5 minutes. Stir regularly, adding more water if they are sticking to the pan. When the onions are soft, add the red pepper and chilli and continue cooking for 3–5 minutes, stirring occasionally.

Drain the mixed beans and sweetcorn and rinse thoroughly. Add them to the pan along with the chopped tomatoes, tomato purée, lime juice, honey/agave syrup, cumin, smoked paprika, allspice, black pepper and salt. Mix all the ingredients well and bring to the boil, then reduce the heat and simmer over a low heat for 5–10 minutes.

Chop the coriander and add just before serving. Serve with rice.

SERVES 4

1 red onion
2 cloves of garlic
1 medium red pepper
1 large fresh red chilli
4 tablespoons water
2 x 400g tins of mixed beans
1 x 340g tin of sweetcorn
2 x 400g tins of good-quality chopped tomatoes
2 tablespoons tomato purée
juice of 1 lime
1½ tablespoons honey/ agave syrup
2 teaspoons ground cumin
½ teaspoon smoked paprika
1 teaspoon ground allspice
¼ teaspoon freshly ground black pepper
2½ teaspoons salt
a bunch of fresh coriander

BURRITOS WITH SPICY COUSCOUS, REFRIED BEANS, CORN GUACAMOLE AND A SOUR CREAM TAHINI MAYO

This is a rockin' recipe – it's a great tactile group/family dinner, with everyone mucking in to make their own burritos just the way they like them. Although there are a few parts to this dish, it takes just twenty minutes to prepare, and all the bits keep for a couple of days in the fridge if they're not eaten on the first go! Goes well served with tzatziki (see page 182).

Put the couscous into a bowl and mix in the cumin, chilli flakes (leave out if you don't want it too spicy), salt and smoked paprika. Pour on boiling water to come about 1cm above the level of the dry couscous. Cover with a lid and leave for 5 minutes.

To make the refried beans, peel and finely chop the garlic. Drain and rinse the beans. Put 2 tablespoons of oil into a frying pan and place on a medium heat. Fry the garlic until it starts to go golden, then add the beans, together with the lime juice, cumin, salt, tamari/soy sauce, black pepper and water. Start to mash lightly with a wooden spoon. Cook for about 4 minutes, then taste to see if you need to adjust the seasoning. Rip up the coriander and add to the mixture.

Now make your guacamole. Chop the avocado flesh into bite-size pieces, quarter the cherry tomatoes, and put both into a big bowl. Rip the coriander, chop the garlic, and add to the bowl with the rest of the ingredients. Mash slightly so everything comes together – adjust the seasoning if you want to, but it should taste great as it is!

To make the sour cream tahini mayo, put all the ingredients into a bowl and mix well with a fork until they reach a mayonnaise-like consistency.

Now it's burrito time! Take your wrap and add the ingredients as you like – roll it into a burrito and eat as is, or heat in a pan till it's warm and starts to crisp up. Enjoy!

MAKES 6

6 wraps or tortillas

For the spicy couscous:
150g wholemeal couscous
1 teaspoon ground cumin
¼ teaspoon chilli flakes
¼ teaspoon salt
½ teaspoon smoked paprika

For the refried beans:
4 cloves of garlic
2 x 400g tins of black beans/ kidney beans
oil
juice of ½ a lime
4 teaspoons ground cumin
½ teaspoon salt
1 tablespoon tamari/soy sauce
½ teaspoon freshly ground black pepper
5 tablespoons water
a small bunch of fresh coriander

For the corn guacamole:
2 ripe avocados
8 cherry tomatoes
a handful of fresh coriander
1 clove of garlic
juice of ½ a lime
½ teaspoon ground cumin
½ teaspoon salt
a pinch of ground chilli
a pinch of freshly ground black pepper, to taste
100g cooked sweetcorn, from a tin

For the sour cream tahini mayo:
4 tablespoons tahini
juice of 1 lime
1 tablespoon honey/maple syrup/ agave syrup
4 tablespoons water

CHOCOLATE CHILLI WITH CORNBREAD

Chocolate is a key ingredient in some mole dishes that come out of Oaxaca in Mexico. Mole (pronounced mo-lay) is the local word for sauce. This recipe is a tasty take on a chilli, with dark chocolate giving it a depth of flavour and adding an air of intrigue to the dish!

Preheat the oven to 180°C/350°F/gas mark 4.

Peel and finely chop the garlic. Slice the leeks into rounds, including the green tops. Deseed the peppers and, if using a fresh chilli, deseed and finely slice it lengthwise. Chop the courgette into bite-size pieces.

Heat the oil in a big saucepan and fry the leeks and garlic on a medium heat for 5 minutes, stirring regularly to make sure they don't burn. Add the courgette and peppers along with the chilli, whole cumin seeds and salt, and fry for a further 5 minutes.

Drain the kidney beans and rinse thoroughly. Add to the pan together with the tinned tomatoes, tomato purée, ground coriander, ground cumin, paprika and black pepper. Turn the heat up to high and bring to the boil, then reduce to a simmer, add the chopped chocolate and leave to simmer for a further 10 minutes.

Finely chop the fresh coriander and mix it into the chilli with the lime juice. Taste and adjust the seasoning if necessary.

To make the cornbread, first mix the ground flax and water together in a small bowl to make 'flax eggs' (see page 253). Leave to sit for 10 minutes.

Mix the rest of the dry ingredients together in a large bowl. In a separate bowl, mix all the wet ingredients, then add the 'flax eggs' and stir in. Add the wet mix to the dry ingredients and mix thoroughly until they form a dough.

Put the chilli into a shallow pie dish (or an approx. 25cm quiche dish), spreading it evenly. Cover the chilli with the spinach leaves. Top it off with the cornbread dough, then put into the preheated oven and bake for 15 minutes.

Serve with a simple green salad and sour cream (or coconut yoghurt if you are dairy-free – see page 19).

SERVES 6

For the chocolate chilli:
2 medium leeks
4 cloves of garlic
2 red peppers
1 whole fresh chilli or ½ teaspoon ground chilli
1 courgette
2 tablespoons oil
1 tablespoon cumin seeds
2½ teaspoons salt
1 x 400g tin of kidney beans
2 x 400g tins of chopped tomatoes
100g tomato purée
1 tablespoon ground coriander
1 tablespoon ground cumin
½ teaspoon smoked paprika
¼ teaspoon freshly ground black pepper
50g dark chocolate (70% best)
a small bunch of fresh coriander
juice of ½ a lime

For the cornbread:
1 tablespoon ground flax seeds
3 tablespoons water
130g fine polenta
85g buckwheat flour/rice flour
2 teaspoons baking powder
½ teaspoon salt
80ml honey/agave syrup
90ml rice milk
60ml rapeseed oil

To assemble:
100g baby spinach

HEARTY SPANISH VEG PAELLA

This is a very tasty vegetable version of the traditional Spanish seafood dish. Instead of the seafood we have used sautéd vegetables and herbs. And to keep your heart smiling we've kept this oil-free and substituted short-grain brown rice for the traditional white paella rice. Great topped with crumbled cashew nuts and olives.

Put the rinsed rice and the stock into a large family-size saucepan. Add the turmeric and mix through the rice – this will give it a lovely yellow colour. Put the lid on, but leave it slightly askew, and bring to the boil. Reduce to a low heat and leave to simmer for 40 minutes. While the rice is simmering, prepare the rest of the paella.

Deseed the peppers and chop these and the courgette into bite-size pieces. Put to one side. Peel and finely chop the onions and garlic. Grate the carrot into a bowl.

Put the garlic and onions into a large saucepan with 4 tablespoons of water. Sauté on a medium heat for 5 minutes, adding more water if they start to stick to the bottom. Add the grated carrot to the pan along with 1 teaspoon of salt and leave to simmer for a further 3 minutes, stirring regularly.

Add the red wine, chopped tomatoes, mixed herbs, black pepper and smoked paprika. Turn up the heat, bring to the boil, then reduce to a simmer for 5 minutes.

Now add the chopped peppers and courgette to the sauce along with the honey, tamari/soy sauce, the remaining teaspoon of salt and the lemon juice. Mix well and cook on a gentle simmer for 15 minutes, or until all the veg are cooked. If you find all the liquid is gone from the veg and the rice is still not cooked, add a little water – preferably boiling – to the veg and mix well.

In the meantime, trim the green beans, cut them in half, and finely chop the parsley.

Once the rice is cooked, add the tomato and veg sauce mix along with the green beans. Cook for a further couple of minutes, mixing everything through. Taste, season with salt and pepper if necessary, and garnish with the chopped flat-leaf parsley and some chilli flakes.

Serve with a simple green salad.

SERVES 4–6

500g short-grain brown rice
1.3 litres vegetable stock
1 teaspoon ground turmeric
3 peppers (1 red, 1 green and 1 yellow)
1 courgette
2 red onions
5 cloves of garlic
1 small carrot
2 teaspoons salt
4 tablespoons red wine
2 x 400g tins of good-quality chopped tomatoes
3 teaspoons dried mixed herbs
½ teaspoon ground black pepper
½ teaspoon smoked paprika
1½ tablespoons honey
2 tablespoons tamari/soy sauce
juice of 1 lemon
100g green beans
a good bunch of fresh flat-leaf parsley
chilli flakes, to garnish

VRON'S EASY QUINOA, STEAMED VEG AND CARAMELIZED ALMOND DINNER

This is one of Elsie and Issy's granny Veronica's staple recipes that Dave has put a twist on. The caramelized almonds will leave you hunting through your bowl looking for more! This dish works great with whatever veg you have, so don't feel restricted to the ones we have used. Great with whatever fresh herbs you have to hand, chopped and added at the end.

Peel and finely chop the onion and garlic, and finely dice the tomato. Peel and grate the ginger.

Finely chop the sweet potato and carrots. Cut the woody ends off the asparagus and discard. Slice the remainder of each spear into three. Thaw the frozen peas by putting them into a bowl and covering them with warm water. Deseed the red pepper and slice into long thin strips.

Put the oil into a large saucepan over a high heat. When the oil is hot, add the onion, tomato, garlic and ginger, and cook for 5 minutes, stirring regularly.

Add the turmeric and curry powder to the pan and stir well. Add the quinoa, vegetable stock, sweet potato, carrots and bay leaves. Bring to the boil, then reduce the heat and put the lid on, leaving it slightly askew to let the steam out.

When the liquid level drops below the top of the cooking quinoa (about 10 minutes), add the asparagus, peas and red pepper, letting them sit on top of the quinoa. Simmer until just about all the water has evaporated (about 5–10 more minutes).

Turn the heat off, put the lid on and leave to sit for about 5 minutes, until the quinoa has puffed up and is really fluffy.

Meanwhile, roughly chop the almonds. Heat a small frying pan on a medium heat and put the almonds into it along with the 3 tablespoons of tamari and 1½ tablespoons of honey/agave syrup. Stir continuously for 4 minutes, or until the almonds start to get golden and the liquid starts to dry up. Watch very carefully, as they will overcook and burn very easily.

Stir the vegetables and quinoa well, squeeze the lemon juice over, and serve with the caramelized almonds on top. Dave loves a sprinkle of chilli flakes over this too.

SERVES 4–6

1 onion
3–4 cloves of garlic
1 tomato
a thumb-size piece of fresh ginger
1 medium sweet potato
3 carrots
½ a bunch of asparagus (about 10 spears)
150g frozen peas
1 red pepper
2 tablespoons oil
1½ teaspoons ground turmeric
2 teaspoons curry powder
275g quinoa
700ml vegetable stock or water
2 bay leaves
juice of ½ a lemon

For the topping:
a handful of whole almonds
3 tablespoons tamari
1½ tablespoons honey/ agave syrup

EASY INDIAN BIRYANI

Dave first ate biryani with Janet's mom, Veronica, out in Melbourne. It was her Indian family recipe and took all day to make. Dave ate enough to sink a ship and has tried multiple times to replicate it! Here is our simpler version, where the rice is cooked in coconut milk (instead of buttermilk) with lots of spices and seeds. It's a lovely wholesome dinner, perfect with the mint raita accompaniment.

Finely chop the tomato, cut the leek and carrots into rounds, and peel and finely slice the garlic. Peel and grate the ginger. Put the frozen peas/edamame beans into a bowl, cover with warm water and leave to thaw.

Put the oil into a large pot on a high heat. Reduce the heat to medium and add the leek, garlic, tomato and grated ginger together with the cumin seeds. Stir continuously for 3–5 minutes, until the garlic starts to turn golden. Add the turmeric, curry powder, whole cardamom pods, cinnamon sticks and bay leaves, and stir for a minute. Now add the coconut milk and cook for a further 3 minutes.

Add the rice to the pot with the vegetable stock, carrots and currants. Put the lid on, bring to the boil, then reduce to a simmer. Leave the lid slightly askew for the steam to escape, and cook until just about all the water has evaporated from the bottom of the pot. You may need to add more water until the rice is cooked through.

Drain the kidney beans and butterbeans and rinse well. Add to the pot along with the drained peas/beans and heat for a further 3 minutes.

For the mint raita, finely chop the mint. Grate the cucumber into a colander, sprinkle with the salt and leave to sit for 5 minutes. Squeeze out the juice. In a bowl, mix the mint with the grated cucumber and all the other raita ingredients.

Once your biryani is ready, roughly chop the coriander and scatter it, along with some pomegranate seeds, over each serving. Serve the raita on the side. Some toasted pitta breads and any type of pickles are also great with this dish, particularly lime or mango pickle.

SERVES 6–8

1 large tomato
1 leek
3 carrots
4 cloves of garlic
a thumb-size piece of fresh ginger
200g frozen peas/edamame beans
2 tablespoons oil
2 tablespoons cumin seeds
1½ teaspoons ground turmeric
2 teaspoons curry powder
4 cardamom pods
2 cinnamon sticks
2 bay leaves
1 x 400ml tin of coconut milk
380g basmati rice
1.3 litres vegetable stock
50g currants/raisins
1 x 400g tin of kidney beans
1 x 400g tin of butterbeans

For the mint raita:
a medium bunch of fresh mint
¼ of a cucumber
a pinch of salt (for salting cucumber)
250ml natural yoghurt of your choice
juice of ½ a lime
½ teaspoon ground cumin
a pinch of freshly ground black pepper

To serve:
a small bunch of fresh coriander
seeds from 1 fresh pomegranate

COCONUT CHANA MASALA WITH SPINACH

Quick, super-tasty and oh so lovely! Traditionally an Indian chana masala doesn't have coconut milk or spinach, but the addition of the coconut gives a creamy texture and the spinach just bumps up the nutritional power. Serve this with brown rice or your grain of choice to bulk it out and soak up the lovely creamy sauce.

Peel and finely chop the onion, garlic and ginger. Deseed and finely chop the chilli (leave the seeds in if you like it hot). Cut the tomatoes into small bite-size pieces.

In a small bowl, mix all the spices together. Drain the chickpeas and rinse well.

Get a large pot and fry the onion, garlic, ginger and chilli in 1 tablespoon of the oil on a high heat for 5 minutes, stirring regularly until the onions are starting to brown and the garlic is turning golden.

Turn the heat down to medium, add the spice mix and salt, and cook for 2 minutes with the remaining tablespoon of oil. There should be a lovely strong aroma in the kitchen!

Next, add the chopped tomatoes and cook for 2 minutes, stirring regularly. Add the coconut milk and chickpeas, bring to the boil and leave to simmer for 15 minutes.

Turn off the heat, stir in the spinach and lime juice, and serve.

SERVES 2–4

1 medium onion
2 cloves of garlic
½ a thumb-size piece of fresh ginger
1 small red chilli
3 tomatoes
1 teaspoon cumin seeds
1 teaspoon ground coriander
1 teaspoon ground cumin
2 teaspoons ground turmeric
2 teaspoons paprika
1 teaspoon garam masala
¼ teaspoon freshly ground black pepper
1 x 400g tin of chickpeas
2 tablespoons oil
1½ teaspoons salt
1 x 400g tin of coconut milk
100g baby spinach
juice of ½ a lime

ANTO'S BEAST BOWL

Anto, who works with us, is also a strength, conditioning and jujitsu coach. He eats weights for breakfast and can even do back flips – he's a beast! This is his optimal post-workout feed to stay metabolically active and keep building muscle and burning fat.

Preheat the oven to 180°C/350°F/gas mark 4.

Peel and finely chop the garlic and ginger. Put these into a blender with the other ingredients for the marinade and whiz until smooth (or chop very finely and mix with a fork if you don't have a blender).

Cut the tempeh into thumb-width slabs. Using a fork, pierce the tempeh, making lots of holes for the marinade to soak into. Line a baking tray with baking parchment. Put the tempeh slabs on the tray and pour over the marinade. Make sure they are thoroughly coated. Put the tray of tempeh into the preheated oven for 10 minutes. Then take out the tray, turn each piece over, and bake for another 10 minutes.

In the meantime, chop the red onion and garlic for the quinoa. Tear or chop the kale (destalked) or other greens into bite-size pieces.

Put the coconut oil into a medium-size pan and heat for a minute. Add the chopped onion and garlic and fry, stirring regularly, for 5 minutes, or until the onions turn translucent. Add the turmeric and mix it into the onions. Add the quinoa and fry it for a couple of minutes, then pour in the vegetable stock. Cover with a lid and bring to the boil, then reduce to a gentle simmer, leaving the lid askew.

Once the water level drops below the level of the quinoa, add the greens to the pot, cover, and cook until nearly all the water has boiled away – add more water if the quinoa is still not cooked. When the quinoa is cooked, remove the pan from the heat and leave to sit for a couple of minutes with the lid on before serving.

For the protein seasoning, finely chop the goji berries with chilli flakes and ground seaweed.

Serve the quinoa with the tempeh slabs on top and sprinkle with the seasoning.

SERVES 2–3 (GENEROUSLY)

1 x 300g block of tempeh

For the marinade:
2 cloves of garlic
a thumb-size piece of fresh ginger
3 tablespoons sesame oil
4 tablespoons tamari/soy sauce
4 tablespoons maple syrup

For the quinoa:
1 red onion
2 cloves of garlic
200g kale or other greens (collard/spinach/chard/cabbage/broccoli)
2 tablespoons coconut oil
1 teaspoon ground turmeric
170g quinoa (if you can get the three-coloured quinoa it looks better)
460ml vegetable stock/water

For the protein seasoning:
2 tablespoons goji berries
1 teaspoon chilli flakes
a few pinches of ground kelp/nori/dulse or other ground seaweed

BLACK BEAN, SQUASH AND ROASTED GARLIC BURGERS

Steve first came up with this recipe while on holiday with the family – it was quick, easy and worked out great on the barbecue. The burgers are super on their own, or served with some homemade ketchup (see page 184) and tzatziki (see page 182) in a pitta or flatbread.

Preheat the oven to 180°C/350°F/gas mark 4.

Peel and deseed the squash, chop into bite-size pieces, then put them on a baking tray with the garlic cloves and ½ teaspoon of the salt. Toss in the oil to coat and put into the oven for 25 minutes. Put the cashew nuts on a separate baking tray and bake in the oven for 10 minutes.

While the squash is baking, drain and rinse the black beans and put them into a large bowl with the juice and zest of the lemon. Chop the coriander and add to the bowl.

Once the squash is soft, take the tray out of the oven. Leave the oven on if you're baking the burgers straight away. Squeeze the garlic cloves out of their skins and chop roughly. Chop the roasted cashew nuts into small pieces. Add the squash, garlic and cashew nuts to the bowl of black beans along with the rest of the salt, the pepper, ground cumin and breadcrumbs.

Use a potato masher to mash the ingredients in the bowl until the flavours are well mixed and marry together – this should take about 5 minutes.

Shape into 6 burger-shaped patties, then bake on a baking tray in the oven for 15 minutes. If you're grilling them on the barbecue, grill for 5–10 minutes each side until firm.

MAKES 6

550g squash (1 medium butternut squash)
5 cloves of garlic
1 teaspoon sea salt
2 tablespoons oil
150g raw cashew nuts
1 x 400g tin of black beans
juice and zest of 1 lemon
50g fresh coriander
¼ teaspoon freshly ground black pepper
1 tablespoon ground cumin
100g breadcrumbs

COURGETTE FRITTERS

Green, tasty and quick to make, with lots of super-fresh flavours. We made these fritters egg-free, using polenta instead to bind them together. They make an easy light dinner or a lovely brunch, served with a simple green salad, some toasted wholemeal pitta breads cut into soldiers and some of our homemade tzatziki (see page 182).

If using frozen peas, soak them in a bowl of warm water, to thaw. Grate the courgettes and put into a colander. Sprinkle a pinch of salt over and leave to sit for about 10 minutes.

In the meantime, peel the garlic, deseed the chilli and chop them finely together with the scallions. Roughly chop the mint and dill.

After 10 minutes, squeeze the courgettes in your hands to remove any moisture. Place the grated courgettes in a large bowl. Crumble the feta into the bowl, then add all the remaining ingredients (except the oil) and mix thoroughly. Heat the oil in a pan and 'test-cook' a small ball of the mixture to see how it holds up. Add some more polenta if it doesn't hold together.

Now take small handfuls of the mixture and flatten them into small fritters. Put some extra polenta on a plate and roll the fritters in it, then, on a medium heat, cook them for a few minutes on each side till they turn golden brown. Turn with care.

Serve with some salad, and tzatziki with some chopped chillies stirred through to add a bit of a kick!

MAKES ABOUT 8 PALM-SIZE FRITTERS

200g fresh or frozen peas
500g courgettes
1 teaspoon salt
2 cloves of garlic
1 red chilli
6–8 scallions
a small bunch of fresh mint
a small bunch of fresh dill
200g feta cheese
2 teaspoons lemon zest
100g polenta, plus extra
  for coating
½ teaspoon freshly ground
  black pepper
1 tablespoon oil

NO-FRY FALAFELS

Originally we called this recipe 'Five-minute Falafels' but after lots of time-trialling we realized that the name was a little misleading! Still, they don't take that long – about fifteen minutes. The addition of the ground flax seed binds them; the coconut concentrate adds a sweetness and richness and the cashews a lovely nuttiness. Serve with your favourite toppings, or stuff them into toasted pittas with hummus (page 175), tzatziki (page 182) or harissa (page 192), grated carrot, red cabbage sauerkraut (page 185), sliced avocado and mixed green leaves.

Preheat oven to 180°C/350°F/gas mark 4.

Drain the chickpeas and rinse thoroughly. Deseed and finely chop the chilli. Finely chop the coconut cream concentrate.

In a food processor, blend all the ingredients – except the chickpeas – until smooth. Add the chickpeas and pulse until blended but still with some small chunks. Taste and season with more salt/pepper/chilli if you think the mix needs it.

Roll the mix into little balls or nuggets – you should get about 20.

Bake them for 20 minutes, until they go nice and crispy on the outside.

SERVES 4 (ABOUT 20 FALAFELS)

2 x 400g tins of chickpeas
½ a fresh green chilli
50g coconut cream
    concentrate (small block)
2 tablespoons ground flax seeds
2 teaspoons ground cumin
a small bunch of fresh coriander
2 cloves of garlic
½ a red onion
1 teaspoon salt
½ teaspoon black pepper
juice of 1 small lemon
50g toasted cashew nuts

GRILLED HALLOUMI BURGER WITH CHILLI KETCHUP AND TAHINI MAYO

This is a fab barbecue recipe and goes down a treat with both veggies and non-veggies – always a winner! It's one of the most popular dishes on our evening menu.

Start by preparing your veg. Cut the courgette in half and then into thin strips lengthwise. Slice the aubergines lengthwise into thin strips. Chop the pepper vertically into four large sections, discarding the core with the seeds. Chop the halloumi into 4 thin rectangular slices.

Put the cut veg into a large bowl with 4 tablespoons of the oil and the salt. Mix well until they all have a nice even coating.

Start to grill the prepared veg on a hot barbecue, turning regularly – you want them nicely charred but also soft and tender.

Remove your cooked veg from the grill and set aside while you cook the halloumi – it will cook very quickly! Put it on the barbecue until it has nice grill marks on each side, about 5 minutes.

Toast the buns on the barbecue, then layer them up with some homemade ketchup on the bottom bun, Happy Pear mayo on the top bun, grilled courgettes, aubergine, halloumi, roasted peppers and some rocket in between. Alternatively you can spread the inside of your toasted pitta pocket with ketchup and mayo on either side and fill with your halloumi, veg and greens. Take the first bite . . . epic, and oh so tasty!

SERVES 2–4

1 courgette
1 aubergine
1 red pepper
5 tablespoons olive oil
1 teaspoon salt
1 x 200g pack of halloumi cheese
4 burger buns or wholemeal pittas
homemade ketchup (page 184)
homemade Happy Pear mayo (page 181)
50g rocket or similar greens

'MEATY' VEGGIE BURGERS

A great entry-level veggie burger! These are packed full of flavour and are really quick to make. Serve in a bun, with some homemade ketchup and mayo (see pages 184 and 181).

Peel and finely chop the ginger and garlic. Dice the tempeh into small cubes.

Put the oil into a large frying pan on a high heat. Add the ginger, garlic, pumpkin seeds and tempeh and fry for 4–5 minutes, keeping everything moving in the pan, until the tempeh is nice and brown and a fab smell wafts up.

Mix together the tamari, honey and sesame oil in a mug and add to the mixture in the frying pan. Cook for a further 3 minutes, then remove from the heat. Add the lime juice and the chopped parsley or coriander.

Drain and rinse your black beans. Put them into a food processor with the fried tempeh mixture and whiz for 1 minute, until smooth – but make sure not to blend for any longer, otherwise too much liquid will be released and the burgers will end up soggy!

Take the blended mixture and shape into 6 burger-shaped patties, using your hands (you may need to mix in some of the oats to dry the mixture as needed, so that the burgers are nice and firm).

Grill or barbecue (or bake in the oven at 180°C/350°F/gas mark 4 for 15 minutes) until cooked through, then sandwich in toasted burger buns or pittas and serve with homemade ketchup and mayo.

MAKES 6 BURGERS

a thumb-size piece of ginger
3 cloves of garlic
1 x 300g block of tempeh
2 tablespoons oil
100g pumpkin seeds
4 tablespoons tamari
3 tablespoons honey
2 tablespoons toasted sesame oil
juice of 1 lime
a small bunch of fresh parsley
   or coriander
1 x 400g tin of black beans
a handful of rolled oats
6 burger buns or wholemeal
   pittas

SPICY MILLET AND MUSHROOM BURGERS

These spicy burgers are lovely and crunchy, with a nice bit of chewiness! Great served with your favourite grilled veggies and tzatziki and homemade ketchup (see pages 182 and 184). They also work great served in buns, along with some potato wedges or a simple green salad.

Preheat the oven to 180°C/350°F/gas mark 4 if you're going to bake these burgers.

Finely slice the chilli (leaving the seeds in, if you want it spicier!).

To cook the millet, put it into a pot with the water, salt, chilli, paprika and cumin. Bring to the boil, then reduce to a simmer until all the water has been absorbed – this should take about 15 minutes. Leave to cool in the pot.

While the millet is cooking, chop the mushrooms into small pieces and peel and finely dice the garlic. Put the oil into a non-stick frying pan on a high heat. Once hot, add the mushrooms, garlic and sunflower seeds, and stir continuously for about 4 minutes.

Mix the honey/agave syrup and tamari/soy sauce together in a cup until all the honey or syrup is mixed in, then add to the frying pan. Cook for a few minutes, until the mushrooms are tender and the tamari and honey mix has all been absorbed. Once cooked, turn off the heat and transfer the mixture to a large bowl.

Chop the mint very finely and add to the bowl with the cooked millet. Mix well together, then shape into 6–8 burger-shaped patties, using your hands. Bake in the preheated oven for 15 minutes. Alternatively grill for 10–15 minutes, turning them halfway to ensure that both sides go lovely and crispy.

MAKES 6–8 BURGERS

1 fresh red chilli
200g millet
900ml water
1 teaspoon salt
2 tablespoons paprika
2 teaspoons ground cumin
200g mushrooms of choice
2 cloves of garlic
2 tablespoons oil
100g sunflower seeds
1 tablespoon honey/agave syrup
4 tablespoons tamari/soy sauce
a small bunch of fresh mint

BLISTERED GRILLED VEG, FETA AND PINE NUT STUFFED PEPPERS

These have to be done on a barbecue – ideally a charcoal one. They're super-tasty, really delicious, easy to make, and look amazing.

Start your couscous by putting it into a large bowl, with a pinch of salt. Pour on enough boiling water to come just above the level of the couscous, then cover with clingfilm and set aside.

Now prepare the veggies. Peel and quarter the onion, and finely slice the courgettes and aubergine lengthwise into thin strips. Put them into a bowl with the sugarsnaps or beans and toss everything in the oil with a pinch of salt.

Grill all the oiled veg on the barbecue, turning often to ensure all sides are done. Remove when soft and nicely charred, then chop them into bite-size pieces.

Next put the whole peppers on to the grill, keeping an eye on them, until each side gets nicely charred. Use tongs to turn them, if you have some.

Roughly chop the coriander and crumble the feta. Add to the cooked couscous along with the chopped grilled veggies and pine nuts/cashew nuts. Mix well, taste and season more if needed.

Once the peppers are looking beautifully charred, cut their tops off and scoop out the seeds, draining out any moisture inside. Using a spoon, stuff each pepper with the couscous mix. They are usually still warm when we eat them, but they can be made in advance and served cold.

SERVES 4–6

150g couscous
salt
1 onion
2 courgettes
1 aubergine
2 tablespoons olive oil
100g sugarsnap peas or
  fine beans
6 peppers
  (a mix of colours is nice)
a small bunch of fresh coriander
200g feta cheese
100g toasted pine nuts/
  cashew nuts

THE VEGGIE BARBECUE 101

We've both been veggies since 2002, and only recently discovered the fun of barbecuing vegetables! Cooking outside, over fire (even if it is gas), you feel connected to the cooking process and really appreciate your food. And most veg cook wonderfully on a barbecue – it brings out their sweetness and the raw heat gives them a lovely charred edge.

WHAT TYPE OF BARBECUE IS BEST?

A charcoal barbecue will add the extra flavour of the wood and smoke to your food that you won't get with gas, and it's our preference. However, we use gas most of the time ourselves, as it's more convenient.

When cooking vegetables on a barbecue, a big grilling area is best. You'll need more space than when cooking meat. Ideally, the bigger the barbecue the better.

OUR FAVOURITE VEGGIES TO BARBECUE

- **AUBERGINES:** One of Steve's favourite veg on the barbecue. Slice them lengthwise about ½cm thick, brush with a little oil and sprinkle with salt, then grill until they go soft and gooey and stripy. They normally take about 5 minutes to cook. They are super-versatile and can be used to make wonderful canapés and rolls (see page 142).

- **COURGETTES:** These can be a little watery, bland and uninteresting, but on a barbecue they really come into their own. The heat seems to release their potential and you get a crispy charred exterior and a warm gooey juicy centre! They take about 5 minutes to cook. They add an extra dimension to a veggie burger, and roll up really well to make fancy canapés (see page 142).

- **PEPPERS:** Sweet bell peppers can often get a bad rep, but like courgettes, when charred and barbecued, they really are at their best. Just slice off the bottom and cut each pepper into 4 sections – giving 4 sides and the bottom. Brush each piece with a little oil, sprinkle with salt and cook on the grill until they start to char and blister. They normally take 6–7 minutes, provided the barbecue is hot. Alternatively, if you are using charcoal, peppers cook wonderfully right inside the coals, where the skin blisters and chars beautifully while the insides remain juicy, sweet and soft. Just put them whole into the charcoal until the skin starts to blister, then brush off the charcoal, rinse and get stuck in!

- **SWEETCORN:** Parboil the ears for 5 minutes first to speed up the cooking time, then cook on the barbecue until they start to brown slightly and the kernels become large, plump and juicy.

- **ASPARAGUS, FRENCH BEANS, SUGARSNAPS, MANGETOUT, FLAT BEANS:** Not obvious barbecue vegetables, but they all work brilliantly – crispy on the outside and soft, sweet and juicy inside! Just toss with a little oil and salt and cook until they start to char and get grill marks.

- **CHERRY VINE TOMATOES:** Put a whole vine on the barbecue and leave until the tomatoes pop – our dad loves to do this. They make any plate they are on look prettier and are warm balls of sweet juiciness . . . nice one, Dad!

- **POTATOES:** Use waxy potatoes and parboil for 10 minutes. Cut into slices about 2cm thick, brush with a little oil, sprinkle with salt, and cook on each side until they start to crisp and brown – barbecued potatoes are like chips with an extra charred dimension!

- **SWEET POTATOES:** Give them a good scrub and cut out any gnarly bits. Cut into wedges and parboil for 10 minutes, then brush with a little oil, sprinkle with salt, and cook until they start to char nicely – they develop a lovely crispy skin that complements their soft sweet interior beautifully!

- **SQUASH/PUMPKIN:** Wash the outside, cut into rounds about 1½cm thick, and parboil for 5 minutes. Grill until they start to char and taste similar to sweet potatoes, with a starchier quality.

AUBERGINE ROLLS

These make a fancy canapé at any barbecue – they really celebrate the wonderfully unique flavour of each vegetable. You can use aubergines or courgettes as the 'wrapping', whichever is handiest.

Light your barbecue.

Cut the red pepper into 5 'slices' (the bottom and 4 sides). Cut the aubergine or courgettes lengthwise into 1cm thick slices. Depending on thickness, you should get 4–6 slices per vegetable. Break off the woody ends of the asparagus spears, or top and tail the beans.

Place the vegetables in a large bowl, drizzle a little oil over them, sprinkle with salt, and mix with your hands to make sure everything is fully coated.

Grill each vegetable until it becomes soft and charred-looking. Peppers first (they will take 6–7 minutes), then aubergines or courgettes (5 minutes), and finally asparagus or fine beans (3–4 minutes). They may take longer, depending on your barbecue.

If using the halloumi, cut it into 4 slices. Grill for about 3–5 minutes (depending on the heat of your barbecue) on one side, then turn it over so that both sides brown nice and evenly.

Slice the avocado in half, then scoop out the flesh and cut into long thin slices.

Cut the grilled red pepper and the halloumi, if using, into strips about 1cm wide.

Lay out a slice of grilled aubergine or courgette on a work surface. Across one end of the slice, lay an asparagus spear or a couple of beans, strips of red pepper and halloumi and a slice of avocado. Roll everything up to make a little parcel.

Repeat to make more parcels with the rest of the veg.

MAKES 12 ROLLS

1 red pepper
2 aubergines or 4 courgettes
a bunch of asparagus/a large handful of fine green beans
olive oil
salt
1 x 200g block of halloumi cheese (optional)
1 ripe avocado

DONAL'S SUNDAY DINNER

Dad is an engineer, but growing up we always thought of him as a businessman. He always worked long days, never eating breakfast, fuelled by coffee, sandwiches and snacks, and finished the day with a big dinner, usually after 8 p.m., just before bed. Over the years he became nice and round, with plenty to hold on to! Health was never on his agenda, he just ate whatever was going, didn't really question what he ate, and tended to defer responsibility for his health to the doctor.

When we were growing up, Mom cooked for us every night and made sure we ate meals together. When it came to Sundays she was worn out feeding four hungry boys all week, so she passed the baton to Dad. He had grown up with a big Sunday dinner being the highlight of the week, when all the family gathered together, and it became our family tradition too.

Our Sunday dinners were long social affairs, with Granny being centre of attention. There was an open door policy. There were usually a few friends, maybe some 'out of town' people one of us had brought along, or a new girlfriend – everyone was welcome! There could be as many as fifteen around the table. As enjoyable as it was, Dad often struggled with sleep on Sundays, as he would get 'meat sweats'!

When we started the Happy Pear in 2004, we had been 'plant powered' for a few years and had been chipping away at Mom and Dad about their eating habits. Dad is very rational and follows reason rather than feelings. We gave him The *China Study* (one the best-selling nutrition titles ever in the USA, which advocates a plant-based diet). As an engineer he loved it – all that data and research! It just made sense to him. He started changing to a more plant-based diet. Mom, by default, followed and they both became more open to embracing healthier ways. In 2008, we bought them a trip to a health centre in the States and this sealed the deal. They came back very much on the same page as us, all about the veg!

After changing their eating habits, Dad wondered what would happen to Sunday dinner? Would it actually survive without the big roast centrepiece? He continued to take charge of it, but now, instead of roast lamb or beef, it became all about fancy veg bakes, lots of oven-roasted root veg with plenty of red onion, garlic and thyme, big hefty salads, roast stuffed aubergines, grilled veg straight off the barbecue. Dad really upped his game and found a passion that had been lying dormant for some time.

As Dad says himself, Sunday dinner is actually better now. Now he really relishes the taste of his food. 'There are so many tastes and foods that I just wasn't aware of a few years back.' The variety of food has increased massively, and Sunday dinner is more of a feast than ever.

In terms of Dad's health today, he says the huge lesson for him is waking up to the fact that his health is his responsibility. Giving up nearly all meat and dairy and eating lots of veg has led to a whole change in lifestyle. He has lost weight. He now takes wheatgrass juice every morning and walks for an hour at 6 a.m. rather than jumping into a car and driving to an office. His complaints about aches and pains in his joints have all stopped, because these have either improved or disappeared. His digestion is also much better, and there are no more meat sweats!

HEARTY BARLEY, LEEK AND THYME STEW

This is a seriously chunky, hearty, flavoursome stew, a one-pot wonder that is easy to make and a great wholesome substantial dinner.

Barley is an old grain, the Irish equivalent of rice, and is really nourishing. Dried kombu is a seaweed you'll find in health food shops and some supermarkets. It's loaded with iodine and minerals, so it's a great addition if you decide to include it.

Rinse and drain the barley and set aside.

Cut the carrots and the leeks (including the green tops) into bite-size pieces. Cut the kombu into small strips (no need for this if you are using arame, as it's usually in very fine strips already).

Peel and roughly chop the garlic and onion, and put into a large family-size pan. Roughly chop the tomatoes, using a serrated knife, then add to the pan together with the water and fry for 5 minutes on a high heat.

Add the chopped carrot and leek, bay leaves, thyme leaves, white wine and lemon juice and cook for a further 5 minutes.

Now add the vegetable stock, barley and kombu/arame (if using). Bring to the boil, then reduce the heat and simmer for 45 minutes, until the barley is cooked through and becomes soft, with a texture like rice.

Drain and rinse the butterbeans and add to the pot. Simmer for a further 3 minutes. Finally season with salt, black pepper and chilli flakes (if you like a bit of spice!). If the stew is too thick, add a little more water.

Serve with some nice chunky bread. If eating the day after it's made, add more liquid and re-season, as the barley will continue to absorb water and thicken the stew.

SERVES 4–6

200g pot barley

2 medium carrots

3 medium leeks

a handful of dried kombu/arame (optional)

3 cloves of garlic

1 onion

4 medium tomatoes

4 tablespoons water

2 bay leaves

leaves from 10 sprigs of fresh thyme

150ml white wine

juice of ½ a lemon

2.5 litres vegetable stock

2 x 400g tins of butterbeans

salt and freshly ground black pepper

chilli flakes

CLAIRE'S DUO POTATO CAKES

These are one of our chef Claire's staples. She often cooks them in the Happy Pear on sunny Sundays when she knows the queue will be out the door – they're quick to make and always go down a treat!

Preheat the oven to 180°C/350°F/gas mark 3.

Wash the regular and sweet potatoes. Boil the regular potatoes (with skins on) in a pot of water with a pinch of salt until they are soft, then drain. Bake the sweet potatoes in the preheated oven until tender (about 20 minutes). Keep the oven on to bake the potato cakes later on.

Once cooled, put the regular and sweet potatoes into a large bowl or the pot you just used to boil the potatoes and mash well together.

In the meantime, peel and finely dice the onions. Put the oil into a frying pan over a medium heat. Once warm, add the onions and sauté until just turning golden and soft. Add to the potato mix.

If using quinoa, cook it according to the instructions on page 255. If using couscous, put it into a bowl and just cover with boiling water, leaving it with a lid over it for 5 minutes, until swollen but not wet. Add a quarter of the quinoa/couscous to the potato mix and keep the rest for coating the cakes.

Wash the spinach/kale (remove the main rib of the kale, if using), and blanch in boiling water until just wilted. Drain, squeeze well, chop finely and stir into the potato mix. Roughly chop the basil leaves and add to the mix along with the cheese, salt and pepper and grated nutmeg.

Mix everything together, then take handfuls of the mixture and roll into 6–8 burger-shaped patties. Mix the paprika with the rest of the quinoa or couscous and spread out on a plate. Roll your cakes in this mix to form a crust. Place the cakes on a baking tray and bake for 15 to 20 minutes, until golden.

Great served with a little parsley, cashew and sun-dried tomato pesto (see page 176), or some romesco pesto (see page 177).

MAKES 6–8 CAKES

800g potatoes, unpeeled
400g sweet potatoes, unpeeled
2 red onions
1 tablespoon olive oil
200g quinoa/wholegrain couscous
200g baby spinach/kale
leaves from 50g fresh basil
250g Cheddar cheese
2 teaspoons sea salt
1 teaspoon freshly ground black pepper
¾ of a fresh nutmeg, grated
1½ tablespoons sweet paprika

NO-MATO BOLOGNESE

A beautiful spaghetti Bolognese without any tomatoes – here we use lentils, stock, red wine, mushrooms and garlic to make a really lovely 'meaty' sauce. The avocado gives a creamy texture, and lemon zest and juice elevate the flavour!

Peel and finely chop the red onion and garlic. Deseed and finely dice the chilli. Slice the mushrooms finely, and grate the carrot.

Drain and rinse the lentils, if using a tin. In a blender or using a stick blender, whiz the lentils, red wine, avocado, agave syrup/honey and vegetable stock together.

To start the sauce, get a large family-size saucepan and put it on a high heat. Once warmed up, put the oil in together with the onion, garlic and chilli. Fry, stirring regularly, until the garlic starts to brown (about 2–3 minutes).

Add the mushrooms, grated carrot and mixed herbs to the pan and cook, stirring regularly, for 2 minutes. Add the tamari/soy sauce and cook for a further 2 minutes, stirring regularly. Pour in the wine, stock, lentil and avocado mixture and bring to the boil. Reduce the heat to a gentle simmer and leave the sauce to reduce for 10 minutes, until it has thickened nicely.

While the sauce is simmering, cook the spaghetti, following the instructions on the pack.

Just before serving, stir the spinach, lemon zest and lemon juice into the sauce and season to taste.

Once the pasta is cooked, drain and divide between bowls, topping with your lovely no-mato Bolognese sauce.

SERVES 4–6

1 red onion
4 cloves of garlic
1 red chilli
200g button mushrooms
1 medium carrot
1 x 400g tin of Puy/green/brown lentils (280g drained weight) or 280g cooked lentils
250ml red wine
½ a ripe avocado
1 tablespoon agave syrup/honey
400ml vegetable stock
2 tablespoons oil
1 tablespoon mixed herbs
4 tablespoons tamari/soy sauce
400g whole-wheat spaghetti
100g baby spinach, washed
zest and juice of ½ a lemon
salt and freshly ground black pepper

VEGAN LASAGNE

This dish started as a wild idea but after the first trial went so well it became a definite. In this lasagne we replace the pasta sheets with baked celeriac, which gives a lovely sweet earthiness. The basil cashew cream is very easy to make and adds a creamy richness.

Put the cashews into 300ml of water and soak for 30 minutes.

Preheat the oven to 180°C/350°F/gas mark 4.

Peel the celeriac and slice it into long strips like sheets of lasagne – about ½cm thick. Mix with 1 tablespoon of oil and a pinch of salt, then lay on two baking trays. Scrub the sweet potato, skin on, and slice into bite-size pieces. Toss with 1 tablespoon of oil and a pinch of salt so the pieces are fully coated, and lay on third baking tray.

Bake the celeriac and the sweet potatoes for 25 minutes, or until soft. Take them out of the oven, but leave it on. Peel and roughly chop the onion and garlic. Chop the chilli finely, removing the seeds if you prefer less heat. Finely slice the mushrooms and the courgette. Chop the sun-dried tomatoes very finely.

Put 2 tablespoons of oil into a large family-size pot over a high heat. Add the onion, garlic and chilli and fry for 4 minutes, stirring regularly until the garlic is golden and the onions are transparent. Add the mushrooms, courgettes and bay leaf and continue to fry for 5 minutes, stirring regularly. Add the wine and reduce for 2 minutes. Then add the chopped tomatoes, sun-dried tomatoes, tomato purée, honey/agave syrup, salt and pepper.

Once the sweet potatoes are cooked, add them to the tomato sauce. Bring to the boil, then allow to simmer on a reduced heat for 20 minutes, stirring occasionally.

To make the cashew cream, drain and rinse the soaked cashews. Whiz in a blender with the other cashew cream ingredients (including the basil stalks) until really smooth.

Cover the base of a large family-size baking dish with half the cashew cream. Over this lay half the baked celeriac, then pour over all the tomato sauce. Make another layer with the rest of the celeriac and finish with the remaining cashew cream. Bake for 15 minutes, until the cashew cream sets and the lasagne has a nice baked appearance.

SERVES 6–8

1 large celeriac (approx. 1kg)
4 tablespoons oil
sea salt
1 medium sweet potato (approx. 400g)
1 medium onion
4 cloves of garlic
1 red or green chilli
200g mushrooms
1 courgette
5 sun-dried tomatoes (not in oil)
1 bay leaf
100ml red wine
2 x 400g tins of good-quality chopped tomatoes
100g tomato purée
1½ tablespoons honey/agave syrup
½ teaspoon salt
¼ teaspoon freshly ground black pepper
a handful of baby spinach

For the cashew cream
200g raw cashews
juice of 1 lime
100ml vegetable stock
150ml olive oil (ideally neutral-tasting – not too acidic)
1 teaspoon salt
¼ teaspoon freshly ground black pepper
50g fresh basil

DARRAGH AND YEŞIM'S RICE PESTO DISH

Our brother Darragh and his beautiful wife Yeşim make this rice dish weekly – it's simple, easy to cook, yet really substantial and satisfying. A good sun-dried tomato pesto is key, and the fresh sprouts give the dish a sense of vibrancy and vitality. You can bulk it up by adding some of your favourite roasted veg, prepared before you start. We have topped it with sunflower sprouts and pea sprouts to make it look more appealing, but Darragh usually makes this simply with sprouted beans and alfalfa sprouts.

Cook the rice according to the instructions on page 255. Once cooked, stir in the sun-dried tomato pesto and tamari/soy sauce, together with the olive oil, and mix well.

Rinse the alfalfa sprouts and sprouted beans and add them to the rice. Quarter the cherry tomatoes and stir them through. If you're using roasted veg, add them as well.

Mix thoroughly. If using, garnish with pea and sunflower sprouts and serve. Enjoy!

SERVES 4–6

500g brown basmati rice
150g sun-dried tomato pesto
4 tablespoons tamari/soy sauce
60ml olive oil
1 x 80g tub of alfalfa sprouts
1 x 150g tub of sprouted beans
8 cherry tomatoes

Optional:
200g of your favourite roasted veg (sweet potato, carrot, pumpkin, squash ...)
a handful of pea and sunflower sprouts, or any other sprouts you have

PAD THAI

One of our favourites, a real crowd-pleaser and always very popular on our evening menu. It's a fresh and zesty delicious meal full of noodles, crunchy veg and flavour. Quick to prepare, light and scrummy!

Finely slice the onion and garlic together with the deseeded chilli (keep the seeds in if you like it extra hot) and put them into a bowl. Peel and finely grate the ginger and add to the bowl.

Deseed the peppers and slice them into long thin strips. Rip the oyster mushrooms into bite-size pieces. Chop the pak choi into bite-size pieces. Put the peppers into a separate bowl from the mushrooms and pak choi (they are added at different times). Set aside.

Put the noodles into a big pot and cover with boiling water, adding a pinch of salt. Cook according to the instructions on the packet. Once cooked, drain, rinse with cold water and put aside.

Put the ingredients for the sauce into a cup or a small bowl. Stir with a fork to combine them well together, making sure the coconut milk is properly mixed in.

Heat 2 tablespoons of oil in a large frying pan or wok. Add the onions, garlic, ginger and chilli, together with the peppers, and sauté for up to 5 minutes, or until the onions start to become translucent and the garlic starts to go golden. Stir regularly, adding a little more water if the onions are starting to stick to the pan.

Now add half the sauce mixture to the pan, along with the oyster mushrooms, and cook for 3 minutes, stirring regularly. Add the pak choi, sugarsnaps, noodles and the remaining sauce, give everything a good stir so that the sauce is well mixed in, and cook for another couple of minutes, until everything is heated through.

Top each serving with rinsed beansprouts, chopped coriander, sesame seeds and cashew nuts, and pickled ginger if using.

SERVES 4

1 red onion

3 cloves of garlic

1 medium red chilli

a thumb-size piece of fresh ginger

1 red pepper

1 yellow pepper

200g oyster mushrooms

1 head of pak choi

4 nests of dried noodles (wholewheat, rice or buckwheat)

2 tablespoons oil

150g sugarsnap peas

For the sauce:

1 x 200ml tin of coconut milk

4 tablespoons tamari

2 tablespoons honey/ agave syrup

juice of 1 lime

For the garnish:

1 pack of beansprouts (approx. 200g)

a small bunch of fresh coriander

3 tablespoons sesame seeds

3 tablespoons roasted, crushed cashew nuts

pickled ginger (optional, see page 184)

JAPANESE FOOD BOWL

This dish was inspired by a place in Venice Beach, LA, that served simple, elegant, clean Japanese-style food in bowls. Try to get hold of the red cabbage sauerkraut or make your own (see page 185) – its colour and sharp taste really elevate the dish. If you can't get the samphire for the salad, use chives instead.

Put your rice on to cook first (see page 255). It will take about 40 minutes, so you may want to wait until it's been cooking for about 15 minutes before you start preparing the rest of the dish.

For the salad, soak the seaweed for 10 minutes in a bowl of cold water to rehydrate it. Grate the carrots into another bowl and pour over the lemon juice to stop them from oxidizing. If the samphire is long, cut it into small pieces.

Make the salad dressing by mixing all the ingredients together in a mug.

Cut your block of tempeh into bite-size cubes. Chop the pak choi into small pieces. To make the tempeh sauce, peel and grate your ginger and put it into a bowl with the tamari, sesame oil and agave syrup. Mix well.

Heat a large non-stick pan on a high heat. Add the tempeh and half the tempeh sauce and cook, stirring continuously, for 2 minutes. Add the rest of the sauce and cook for a further 4 minutes.

Add the chopped pak choi to the pan and cook for 2 minutes. Finally, add the spinach and stir for a further minute, until it has wilted. Remove from the heat and leave to one side.

Once the brown rice is cooked, divide between deep bowls along with some tempeh, greens and sauerkraut. Drain the seaweed and assemble the salad ingredients in a bowl. Add the dressing and mix, then add some of the salad to each rice bowl. Enjoy!

SERVES 4

320g short-grain brown rice

For the salad:
10g arame or other dried
    seaweed, finely chopped
3 carrots
juice of ½ a lemon
40g samphire

For the salad dressing:
1 tablespoon rice vinegar/apple
    cider vinegar
2 tablespoons sesame oil
1 tablespoon tamari/soy sauce
½ tablespoon agave syrup

For the tempeh:
1 x 300g block of tempeh
½ a head of pak choi
100g baby spinach

For the tempeh sauce:
½ a thumb-size piece of
    fresh ginger
4 tablespoons tamari/soy sauce
2 tablespoons sesame oil
3 tablespoons agave syrup

To serve:
red cabbage sauerkraut or
    regular sauerkraut

EASY JAPANESE VEG AND NOODLE RAMEN

Ramen is the most popular dish nowadays in Japan. It's an easy and fresh-tasting soupy dish with noodles that's really nourishing, while being a substantial clean dinner. It doesn't matter what type of noodles you use – we usually use brown rice noodles or wholewheat noodles. To make your ramen even better, add some dried seaweed, such as arame, and 2 tablespoons of miso to your broth, and fresh coriander and pickled ginger to the topping.

First make your broth. Peel and grate the ginger. Put the vegetable stock into a large pot with 2 tablespoons of the tamari, the grated ginger, the juice of 1 lime and 1 tablespoon of honey/maple syrup/agave syrup and bring to the boil.

Wipe the mushrooms clean and tear them into bite-size pieces. Mix the remaining 3 tablespoons of tamari, the lime juice and remaining 1 tablespoon of honey in a cup or bowl with the water, then transfer into a separate pan on a medium heat. Add the mushrooms and cook, stirring occasionally, for about 5 minutes, or until the mushrooms have absorbed all the sauce and taste great.

Once your broth is boiling, add the noodles and cook according to the instructions on the packet.

In the meantime, start preparing your toppings. Deseed and finely slice the red chilli, together with the scallions (they're nice sliced at an angle). Grate the carrot and rinse the beansprouts.

Once the noodles are cooked, take them out of the broth with a slotted spoon, dividing them between four deep bowls. Ladle the broth into each bowl so it is just slightly covering the noodles.

Now add the toppings – beansprouts, mushrooms and grated carrot on each side of each bowl, with the chopped scallions, chilli and sauerkraut (if using) in the centre. Finally, sprinkle with sesame seeds.

SERVES 4

a thumb-size piece of
  fresh ginger
2 litres vegetable stock
5 tablespoons tamari/soy sauce
juice of 2 limes
2 tablespoons honey/maple
  syrup/agave syrup
300g oyster mushrooms (button
  mushrooms also work fine)
3 tablespoons water
4 nests of dried noodles

For the toppings:
1 red chilli
4 scallions
1 large carrot
200g beansprouts
sauerkraut (to taste, optional)
sesame seeds

RAINBOW VEG TERRINE

This rainbow-coloured take on the traditional French terrine requires no special ingredients or cooking equipment (apart from a large loaf tin – a 2 or 3lb tin works well), and can be made with whatever you have in your fridge. The feta cheese through the middle of it adds a nice depth of flavour. The terrine sits in the fridge overnight and is served cold. Great served with a few side dishes or a couple of dips and some nice bread.

Preheat the oven to 200°C/400°F/gas mark 6.

Cut the courgettes in half and cut crosswise into strips about ½cm thick. In strips, thinly slice off the outside purple skin from the aubergine and discard the rest. Place the sliced courgettes and aubergine skins in a bowl. Add 1 teaspoon of salt and 2 tablespoons of oil and mix to coat all the veg evenly.

Peel the butternut squash, cut in half lengthwise, remove any seeds and slice lengthwise into 1cm strips. Slice the carrots lengthwise. Put the squash and the carrot strips into a separate bowl along with ½ teaspoon of salt and 2 tablespoons of oil, and mix thoroughly, coating everything evenly.

Slice the peppers into long strips and place in another bowl with 2 tablespoons of oil and ½ teaspoon of salt. Mix thoroughly, coating everything evenly.

Place the vegetables on three separate baking trays and bake in the oven for 20 minutes, or until they are baked/grilled really well. They should smell fab and look slightly charred.

Meanwhile, remove the stalks from the chard, spinach or cabbage (and the main central cabbage vein if using). Bring a medium pot of water to the boil and blanch the greens for about 1 minute. Remove when they are pliable and bright green and rinse under the cold tap to halt the cooking process.

cont'd➡

SERVES 4

2 courgettes
1 aubergine
sea salt
7 tablespoons oil
550g butternut squash
2 carrots
2 red peppers
200g chard/large leaf spinach/ cabbage leaves
1 x 400g tin of black beans
2 cloves of garlic
100g pesto of your choice (parsley, cashew and sun-dried tomato pesto, page 176, goes well)
200g feta cheese

Line a 2 or 3lb loaf tin with clingfilm, so it will be easy to take out the terrine. Dry the chard leaves with kitchen paper and use them to line the tin, overlapping them slightly, leaving enough hanging over the sides to be able to fold it back over the terrine once you've layered it. Reserve a few leaves for later.

Drain and rinse the black beans; peel and finely slice the garlic. Put a small pan on a high heat. Once hot, reduce the heat to medium and add 1 tablespoon of oil. Add the garlic and stir continuously, until golden, then add the black beans. Cook for a further 2 to 3 minutes, then remove from the heat and mash them all together with a potato masher.

When all the veg are baked, remove from the oven and leave to cool. Once they are cool, you can start to layer up your terrine.

As this is a rainbow terrine, start by layering the bottom of the lined tin with the red peppers. Now add a couple spoons of pesto on top and spread it over the top of the red pepper layer (quite like a thin layer of butter in a sandwich).

Next layer up the carrots, pressing them down with a potato masher or flat spatula (or with a tin of something) to even them out and packing the layers tightly. Now 'butter' on a thin layer of pesto.

Now add the squash layer. Continue to press down the terrine after each layer – this is key to keeping your terrine tight and compact once sliced.

Crumble in the feta next and spread out evenly to make the next layer. Repeat with the courgettes, press down, 'butter' with some pesto, then add the aubergine strips. Press down to compact, add another layer of pesto and finally a layer of evenly spread mashed black beans.

Press down one last time, then fold the chard leaves tightly over the bean layer, filling in the gaps with any remaining chard or greens. Wrap tightly with clingfilm. Find something heavy (like a couple of tins) to sit as a weight on top of your terrine and put into the fridge for at least 4 hours. Keep refrigerated until ready to serve.

Turn the terrine out on to a board or large plate, using the clingfilm to help lift it out. Remove the clingfilm, then slice the terrine and serve with a drizzle of pesto on top.

SAVOURY SWISS ROLL

This is one of Juan's dishes. It's quite a common Spanish dish and very versatile – you can fill it with lots of different things. Here we roll up some roasted veg, rocket, Happy Pear mayo (see page 181) and pickled ginger (see page 184). You could also use ketchup (see page 184), or add some of your favourite cheese, grated.

Preheat the oven to 170°C/325°F/gas mark 3. Line a rectangular flapjack-size baking tray with a sheet of baking parchment.

Cut all your veg for roasting into bite-size pieces, put them on a second baking tray and add some salt and oil. Bake in the oven for 20 minutes, until they are softened and beginning to char on the edges. Set aside to cool.

Crack the eggs into a large bowl, add the honey/agave syrup and beat with an electric hand blender for about 25 minutes, until you get a sticky, foam-like consistency. (Yes, it's a lot of beating but it takes this long to get the correct consistency. The end result is worth it!)

Sieve the flour into the bowl, folding it gently through a little bit at a time.

Spoon the mixture into the lined flapjack tray and spread it out evenly. Bake in the preheated oven for 12 minutes, until the top is golden. Set aside until the sponge is cold, then peel the paper off. Turn the oven up to 180°C/350°F/gas mark 4.

Put the sponge on a board with the dark side facing up and spread with the mayo. Add the rocket, the roasted vegetables and the pickled ginger and roll it up carefully, trimming any ragged bits off either end to present it nicely. Cut into chunky slices and serve. Great with a sharp green salad!

cont'd ⇒

SERVES 4–6

5 eggs, preferably free-range or organic

1 tablespoon honey/agave syrup

5 tablespoons white spelt flour (or any white flour)

200g vegetables for roasting (aubergines, peppers, onions, courgettes)

1 teaspoon salt

1 tablespoon olive oil

40g Happy Pear mayo

30g rocket

10g pickled ginger

1. BEFORE ROLLING . . .

2. AFTER ROLLING . . .

CHANGING YOUR LIFE THE HAPPY PEAR WAY

We started our Happy Heart course in 2008 because we wanted to put our faith in the power of eating more veg to the test. And we wanted to see if the research we had been reading would work for everyone, starting with our community in Greystones.

Eight years on, and thousands of participants later, we can say that our four-week programmes have been a huge success. From the start we wanted to measure results – first, to prove to ourselves we were on the right track and, second, to convince the participants that what we were promoting was not some hippy-dippy waffle. We have seen people turning up looking very sceptical (often because they've been pushed into coming or dragged along) and barely hiding their horror at the thought of eating a plant-based diet for a month. On the first night we have a nurse on hand to measure participants' weight, blood pressure and cholesterol levels. We measure again at the end, and if people have been following the programme, the results are fantastic. We have on average a 20 per cent drop in cholesterol in just four weeks, and some people lose as much as 15kg. People are nearly always so amazed and excited about how much better they feel.

We are not trying to force anyone to become vegetarian or vegan. The course is about people experiencing what it feels like to eat a veg-centred diet for four weeks, about breaking bad habits and forming better ones. Here are two of our recent participants.

AUVEEN LUSH

'I was always a fussy eater. Plain, white, no food touching. I could eat boiled eggs for breakfast, lunch and dinner. Food was an inconvenience. Fast food was my idea of heaven – fast, over and done with and full quickly. I was always sporty and happy, slim and fit-looking. I could eat whatever I liked and never get fat.

'But I guess I always wondered how long I could get away with eating the way I did. In the end it caught up with me: in 2014, aged forty-three, I was diagnosed with breast cancer. By then I had two kids who were eight and five. I had a lot at stake. I dealt with the cancer in my own way: OK, what do I have to do? Head down. Get through. When I came out the other side I thought a lot about my relationship with food. I searched for a new way of eating but how was I going to do it? I hated vegetables and could just about tolerate fruit.

'It was Christmas and my husband, Lush, booked me and my sister Ciara on to the Happy Heart course. It was something I would never have done in a million years. Panic set in. Those Happy Pear guys just eat fruit and veg! I wasn't too sure what Lush had signed me up for, and looking back I think I was better off not knowing!

'The first night I sat there in shock, but leaving that night I thought, "Sure I might as well give this a go. It's only four weeks."

'One of the course guidelines is to reduce fat to under 10 per cent. As I had just had an operation the week before starting, I decided to keep the "good fats" in my diet. Stephen didn't mind and said that my cholesterol/weight would just reduce more slowly than someone who was sticking to the less-than-10-per-cent-fat rule. I loved that – that he was OK with me not sticking rigidly to the course; he was just delighted that I was trying it, eating more fruit and vegetables. Total respect.

'The day before that last class, I was in the Happy Pear shop. David was there and he said, "Hey Auv, this is it. One more day and it's finished – woohoo!" I looked at him and said, "No, no, it can't be the end. It's just the beginning." I was hooked.

'My struggle continues every day but I have great support in Lush, my sister Ciara and friend Elena. I might not be good at the science bit of all of this yet, and I'm still learning what I need for a balanced diet, but I now know I don't need every meal to have meat in it. My cholesterol dropped by 20 per cent and remains down, I lost weight and I now enjoy my meals. I have low days and I reach for the chocolate (and not the healthy dark variety!), but I keep thinking this is a long journey, not a sprint, and I'll always have the Happy Pear.'

Auveen's favourite dish is: 'Anything from the Happy Pear that I don't have to cook!'

AMORY SCHWARTZ

Amory, who's fifty-four, is from Philadelphia and has lived in Ireland the last twenty years. He grew up with a traditional eastern European Jewish diet, things like chopped liver and schmaltz (melted chicken fat put into a maple syrup pourer and used as a 'gravy' – no joking!). As a young man he played a lot of sport and ate everything. He also had a big sweet tooth and not much discipline. As he got older he struggled with his weight and it was not a shock to be diagnosed with Type 2 diabetes at forty-eight. He tried diets but his blood test results didn't show any improvement. Any weight he lost, he regained.

In the autumn of 2014 Amory had a reality check. He was in hospital for a weekend with a finger infection. 'The nurse told me that diabetes makes recovery from anything more complicated. I had a freak-out moment then and there.' Amory realized he truly wanted to be healthier.

'While I was moaning to my wife [Kate] about not having a plan to lose weight, eat better, etc. she started serving me Happy Pear food because she was taking the Happy Heart course. I lost a stone over a few weeks and got worried that there was something wrong with me! I didn't think I was on a diet. I felt better and had to buy new clothes (yay!) but I didn't really connect the HH diet to my weight loss. It was only when I started reading the Happy Pear book that the light bulb went off.

'Instead of having meat six days a week, it was down to twice, then once, per week. I didn't miss it, and the burger, when I had it, was so much more enjoyable. I still had my sweets and chocolates, but three times a week instead of twice a day.'

After over six months of eating this way, Amory went to his GP for a regular check-up. 'Normally, I would call to rearrange my appointment for a month hence so that I would have a chance to crash diet before my blood test. This time [May 2015], I couldn't wait for my blood test and to get on the scales. The nurses and the doctor were incredibly happy with my results: had this been my first blood test they would not have considered me to be someone with Type 2 diabetes.

'If people are asked which they would prefer – live like a monk till a hundred or live till sixty-five partying, most people would pick sixty-five. This is the decision people think they are making with eating healthily. But eating this way is not prescriptive. You can cut it up how you like it. It's not like the minute you eat a piece of chicken you are off the team. And it's a virtuous circle: feel better, eat better, lose more weight, feel better.'

Amory loves the chocolate, nut and caramel bars (see page 212). 'They taste so much better than the actual ingredients – they taste like success!'

SNACKS, DIPS & FABULOUS EXTRAS

CARROT HUMMUS

BEETROOT HUMMUS

BASIC HUMMUS

HUMMUS THREE WAYS

This is a really cool thing to do with hummus – make a basic hummus and then vary it! You have one third basic hummus, turn a third of it into a roasted carrot hummus, and another third into a pink sweet beetroot and olive oil hummus. Dave's youngest daughter, Issy, is a serious fan of hummus – she calls it 'butter'! Her favourite is beetroot hummus. If you make these, let us know your favourite on Twitter.

Preheat your oven to 200°C/400°F/gas mark 6.

Cut your carrots into bite-size pieces and put them at one end of a baking tray. Sprinkle with salt and drizzle with a little of the oil.

Remove the dirt from the beetroot, top and tail, then scrub the skin, but don't peel. Roughly chop your beetroot into bite-size pieces, then put them at the other end of the same baking tray and similarly sprinkle with salt and drizzle with a little oil. Keep the beetroot and carrot separate, though – you don't want the colours to merge. Put the baking tray into the preheated oven for 20–30 minutes, or until the veg are well roasted and slightly charred around the edges.

Peel the garlic, drain and rinse the chickpeas, then put into a food processor together with the rest of the basic hummus ingredients. Blend for about 3 minutes, until pretty smooth. This is your main batch of really tasty standard-issue hummus. Taste and season with more salt and pepper if you think it needs it. Divide into 3 equal batches and leave one of the batches aside – this will be your basic hummus.

Once the carrots and beetroot are roasted, take them out of the oven. Put the second batch of hummus into the food processor with the roasted carrots and 2 tablespoons of olive oil, and blend until smooth. Remove and clean out the food processor.

Finally, put the third batch of hummus into the food processor together with the roasted beetroot and 2 table-spoons of olive oil, and blend until smooth.

MAKES ABOUT 1KG

Basic hummus:
5 cloves of garlic (approx. 20g)
3 x 400g tins of chickpeas
150ml lemon juice (juice of 3 lemons)
6 tablespoons light tahini
2½ teaspoons sea salt
a pinch of freshly ground black pepper
½ teaspoon ground cumin
9 tablespoons water

To transform your hummus:
3 medium carrots (250g)
sea salt
6 tablespoons olive oil
1 medium raw beetroot (175g)

PESTO THREE WAYS

SPRING GREEN CASHEW PESTO

MAKES ABOUT 500G

100g York cabbage/
 spinach/chard
3 cloves of garlic
100g raw cashew nuts
200ml olive oil
1 teaspoon sea salt
juice of ½ a lime

This wonderfully creamy green pesto goes great with pasta and tastes like a healthy green carbonara sauce!

Wash your greens. If using chard or York cabbage, remove the fibrous stalks. Peel the garlic.

Dry roast your cashews in a pan on a medium heat until they start to colour.

Blanch your choice of green leaves in boiling water for 4 minutes, until soft, then remove to a plate using a slotted spoon – no need to dry the greens, as a little water will make a more liquidy pesto.

Blend in a food processor with the garlic, cashew nuts, oil, salt and lime juice until you get a smooth creamy delicious texture.

If you are using this as a pasta sauce, chilli flakes and ground pink peppercorns are a great addition.

PARSLEY, CASHEW AND SUN-DRIED TOMATO PESTO

MAKES ABOUT 220G

50g sun-dried tomatoes
3 cloves of garlic
50g raw cashew nuts
50g fresh parsley
juice of 1 lemon
100g rapeseed oil
⅓ teaspoon salt

The combination of the tang of the sun-dried tomatoes and garlic, the creaminess of the cashews and the zestiness of the lemon juice makes this a rocking pesto! It's great on bread, in sandwiches, on pasta – or just eaten off a spoon!

Put the sun-dried tomatoes into a bowl of boiling water and leave to soften for 5 minutes. Peel the garlic.

Toast the cashew nuts in a medium hot frying pan for 8–10 minutes, until they start to brown lightly.

Drain the sun-dried tomatoes, then put them into a blender together with the rest of the ingredients and blend until smooth.

ROMESCO PESTO

SPRING GREEN CASHEW PESTO

PARSLEY, CASHEW AND SUN-DRIED TOMATO PESTO

ROMESCO PESTO

MAKES ABOUT 400G

3 red peppers
2 heads of garlic
150g whole almonds
1 tablespoon cider vinegar
1 teaspoon salt
¼ teaspoon freshly ground
   black pepper
½ teaspoon smoked paprika
2 teaspoons sweet paprika
10 tablespoons olive oil

Romesco sauce is a famous Catalan recipe, based around almonds, garlic and red peppers. This is a combination of two versions of the sauce – our Spanish head chef Juan's, and Dave's. Ours is more like a pesto than a sauce, and works brilliantly wherever you'd use a pesto. Our romesco is lovely over pasta.

Preheat oven to 180°C/350°F/gas mark 4.

Slice the sides and ends off the peppers and remove the seeds. Put the pepper slices on a baking tray. Remove the outer layers from the garlic heads, then slice the top off each head, leaving the tips of the cloves exposed (this makes it easier to get the cloves out once roasted), and place on the same tray as the peppers. Spread the almonds on a separate baking tray.

Put both baking trays into the oven. The almonds will be ready after 10–12 minutes, so remove them from the oven (when they start to darken and smell lovely and roasty). Leave the peppers and garlic in the oven so they roast for 30–35 minutes in total, or until the peppers start to char around the edges.

Once the garlic is cool enough, squeeze out the flesh. In a food processor, blend the roasted almonds, peppers, roasted garlic and all the other ingredients, apart from the olive oil, until smooth – about 7 minutes. Slowly add the olive oil, blending continuously. Taste and add more pepper and salt if necessary

All three pestos will keep in the fridge for up to a week.

TWO NEW TAKES ON PESTO PASTA

SPRING GREEN CASHEW PESTO AND SPAGHETTI CARBONARA

1 x 500g pack of wholegrain spaghetti

500ml spring green cashew pesto (see page 176)

For the garnish (optional):
whole pink peppercorns
chilli flakes

Our wonderfully creamy nutritious green pesto goes amazingly with pasta and your dish will taste like a healthy green carbonara! A super simple dinner, ideal for midweek.

Cook the spaghetti according to the packet instructions. When cooked, drain in a colander and put it back into the pot.

Mix the pesto into the spaghetti. Garnish with pink peppercorns and chilli flakes. And that's it – it's ready to serve!

ROMESCO PASTA

1 x 500g pack of wholegrain spaghetti, or pasta of your choice

400ml romesco pesto

olive oil

salt and freshly ground black pepper

For the garnish (optional):
chilli flakes
fresh basil/rocket leaves
grated/crumbled cheese

Another brilliantly easy quick midweek supper option if you have the romesco pesto already made. And if you don't, it doesn't take that long! Quantities here again are for four, but this recipe and the last are easily adapted to feed just one person or many more than four!

Cook the pasta according to the packet instructions. When cooked, drain it in a colander and put it back into the pot.

Mix the pesto into the pasta, adding some olive oil to help spread the sauce. Taste and season if necessary.

Garnish with chilli flakes, basil/rocket leaves, and, if you are into cheese, Parmesan (or any hard cheese) would taste great here too, as would feta or goat's cheese. And that's it – it's ready to serve!

HAPPY PEAR MAYO

This is a creamy, fatty mayo – very like the 'real' thing! It's easy and makes most things taste great. It goes brill with burgers or in any sandwich!

Preheat the oven to 180°C/350°F/gas mark 4.

Put the garlic cloves (in their skins) on a baking tray and roast for 10 minutes, until soft.

Squeeze the garlic cloves out of their skins into a blender, along with all the other ingredients except the olive oil and blend for 1 minute. Then, keeping the blender running, slowly add the oil until the mix emulsifies.

MAKES ABOUT 650ML

2 cloves of garlic
300ml soya milk
3 tablespoons lemon juice
¾ teaspoon salt
¼ teaspoon freshly ground black pepper
1½ tablespoons Dijon mustard
300ml olive oil

GARLIC TAHINI MAYO

This is a really tasty, healthy spin on garlic mayonnaise. It only takes a minute to make and will add plenty of flavour to a multitude of foods!

Finely chop the garlic, then put it into a small bowl and mix well with the rest of the ingredients. You can also whiz the lot in a blender if you like.

If it's too thick add more water. If it's too thin add more tahini. It should be a thick mayo-like consistency.

MAKES ABOUT 150ML

2 cloves of garlic
4 tablespoons tahini
5 tablespoons water
juice of ½ a lime
a decent pinch of salt
½ tablespoon agave syrup

TZATZIKI

This is a great dip to add to any mezze platter – it goes so well with falafels and spicy food, to cool and freshen things up. The key to making this as traditional as possible is to use Greek yoghurt. To make it dairy-free, use soya yoghurt.

Finely grate the cucumber into a colander, sprinkle with salt and leave to sit for 5 minutes.

Meanwhile, very finely slice the garlic or put through a garlic press. Remove the mint or dill leaves from the stalks and chop very finely.

Squeeze all the liquid out of the cucumber. Mix all the ingredients together in a bowl and season with salt, pepper and a touch of lime juice to taste.

MAKES ABOUT 650G

200g cucumber
salt and freshly ground
 black pepper
1 clove of garlic
15g fresh mint or dill (whichever
 you prefer, or both)
480g yoghurt
juice of ½ a lime

HAPPY PEAR HARISSA

Harissa is a rocking hot paste with its roots in Tunisia. There really is no one perfect version of it. Ours is sweet, spicy, salty and delicious and goes well with everything. You can use it on its own as a dip, or as an ingredient to spice up other dishes. Kept in an airtight jar or tub, it will last for at least two weeks in your fridge. If you like it more sweet than spicy, replace some of the chillies with sun-dried tomatoes.

Preheat the oven to 220°C/425°F/gas mark 7.

Chop the tops off the chillies and cut them in half lengthwise, leaving the seeds in. Roast in the preheated oven for 10 minutes.

Soak the sun-dried tomatoes in boiling water for 5 minutes, then drain.

Once the chillies are done, put them into a food processor together with the drained sun-dried tomatoes and the rest of the ingredients, and blend until smooth.

MAKES 125ML

5 fresh red chillies
40g sun-dried tomatoes
2 cloves of garlic
1 teaspoon chilli flakes
4 tablespoons olive oil
1½ teaspoons sea salt

HAPPY PEAR KETCHUP

Once you've tried this you'll never want to use shop-bought ketchup again!

Mix all the ingredients in a bowl until smooth and well blended. If you want to spice it up, add the red chilli, chopped, seeds and all.

Enjoy as a dip or in your burger!

MAKES ABOUT 400ML

1 x 200g tube of good-quality tomato purée
90g maple syrup/agave syrup
6 tablespoons white wine vinegar/apple cider vinegar
5 tablespoons water
1 teaspoon sea salt

Optional:
1 red chilli

PICKLED GINGER

Most pickled ginger includes preservatives and colourants. This recipe has neither and we use beetroot juce for the colour. Great on burgers, noodles and rice dishes.

Sterilize the glass jar by pouring boiling water into it, then discarding the water.

Peel the ginger and slice very thinly using a mandolin. If you don't have a mandolin, use a potato peeler or a knife. Put the ginger slices into the jar.

Mix the vinegar, salt and agave syrup in a small pan and bring to the boil. Pour the vinegar mix into the jar of ginger and add the beetroot juice (this is only for colour, it won't give any flavour). Top up the jar with hot water. Make sure all the ginger is covered.

As soon the mix cools down, put on the lid and refrigerate. It will be ready to eat in 3 days, but you can eat it before then if you don't mind a bit of a bite. Wait longer if you prefer a soft texture. The flavours improve with time. It will keep for about a month in the fridge.

MAKES A 200ML JAR

150g fresh ginger (the bigger the piece, the better, as it will be easier to slice)
100ml rice vinegar/ any other clear vinegar
½ teaspoon salt
30ml agave syrup
10ml beetroot juice (from cooked beetroot)

RED CABBAGE SAUERKRAUT

An amazing food for your gut – fermented cabbage! This is a recipe from a dear friend of ours, April Dannan from West Cork. She is the queen of fermenting, and she does regular fermentation workshops in the Happy Pear. We use this in our Japanese food bowl (page 158) and falafels (page 128).

Remove a few outer leaves from the cabbage and set aside. Grate the cabbage into a bowl (or grate in a food processor). Lightly season with the salt and massage it into the cabbage for a minute, to start it breaking down.

Put the cabbage into a 2 litre jar, pressing it down with a wooden spoon. You want it to start releasing its juices.

Peel and finely slice the garlic clove and add to the jar, along with the apple cider vinegar. Tightly compress the cabbage, using a wooden spoon, and pour in the water, making sure it comes just above the level of the cabbage.

Finally, top with the cabbage leaves you put aside earlier. These will keep the grated cabbage submerged under the liquid.

Leave the jar in a cool dark cupboard, ideally for 30 days, though it should be fine to eat after a few days. Taste to see. The longer you leave it, the more healthy bacteria will form. You can keep it for up to a year in the fridge, provided you keep the grated cabbage submerged.

MAKES A 2 LITRE JAR

2 heads of red cabbage
½ teaspoon salt
1 clove of garlic
3 tablespoons apple cider vinegar
spring water (chemical-free water)

You will also need a 2 litre jar

JAN'S TOP TIPS FOR FEEDING CHILDREN

When David asked me to write this part of the book I hesitated. After all, I might be out of touch with what it's like to feed a family because I have a whole health shop at my disposal. Then I realized that it's simple: I have two healthy kids who love to eat (good stuff and junk) and if I share what I do it might help other people.

No doubt being around the Happy Pear makes it easier for me to integrate healthy food into our daily lives. But learning about food and how it improves health – physically, mentally and emotionally – has always been a central part of my life. And that's important. Parents being interested in food is key to bringing up children with a good attitude to food. Kids are masters at knowing when you're not walking the talk. I'd never expect my girls to eat something I wouldn't eat myself.

Getting children to eat well and to make healthy food choices is a process. Making food about much more than just the actual eating is key to developing their interest and tastes.

So down to the nuts and bolts. These are the things I do regularly to make sure they are getting what they need:

BREAKFAST

After a vegetable super juice or a smoothie, nine mornings out of ten we eat porridge. I soak it the night before (in half water and half nut/oat/rice milk) in the pot I'm going to cook it in, so I can flick on the stove before I jump in the shower. Soaking it makes it easier to digest and it's also easier for the body to assimilate the vitamins and minerals in it. What we put on top varies, but it's generally any of the following: bee pollen, goji berries, hemp seeds, flax seeds, chia seeds, sunflower seeds, mulberries, fresh fruit, nuts. There are pretty much endless possibilities, which makes it feel as though you're not eating the same thing every day.

Sometimes that can all seem like a bit of a palaver and instead they'll get granola or Weetabix with nut or oat milk and some good stuff (any of the things we have on porridge) thrown on top.

'Learning about food and how it improves health – physically, mentally and emotionally – has always been a central part of my life. And that's important. Parents being interested in food is key to bringing up children with a good attitude to food. Kids are masters at knowing when you're not walking the talk. I'd never expect my girls to eat something I wouldn't eat myself.'

JUICE

This is pretty straightforward. As soon as the kids were on solids and able to drink from a cup with assistance I gave them vegetable juice every morning. It doesn't really matter what time of the day you do it, but it's taken into your system really quickly on an empty stomach and it's good to start off their digestion for the day on something liquid.

They brush their teeth shortly afterwards as part of the morning routine, which stops the enamel on their teeth being damaged from the starches in veg (drinking it from a straw makes this less of a problem).

I don't really recommend juicing fruit because it spikes blood sugar levels and is REALLY bad for teeth. Using carrots, beetroot, cucumber, fennel, and not putting in too much of the bitter stuff (pak choi, celery, chard, kale), it can be really tasty. If they won't drink it to begin with, you can add a kiwi (they are less sweet) or a little apple to sweeten it and gradually reduce the amount of fruit as their palates adjust to the taste.

SMOOTHIES

Again, this one's not rocket science. There are some smoothie recipes earlier (pages 16–17) that the kids love. Again, I steer clear of fruit – it's asking for tooth trouble, and having them accustomed to such sweet drinks is a habit I'd rather avoid. Avocados, spinach, milled flax seeds, goji berries . . . there's no end to what you can throw in there. Playing around with them yourself you'll find combinations that are delicious and you'll learn the right balance of ingredients to get it tasting good, rather than something made from the contents of the compost bin.

These never replace meals in our house but are great as snacks, and the kids love being involved in making them when you have time to involve them. They're always far more inclined to eat or drink things they've made themselves!

SNACKS

The cupboard and fridge always have some basic stuff in them so that I can quickly make healthy snacks for the kids with no prep time at all. Nuts, crackers, oat biscuits, rice cakes, tahini, nut butters and a full fruit bowl mean I have almost insta-snacks. When it comes to fruit the kids eat whole fresh fruit because the sugar in it is released more slowly than in juice and it's high in fibre.

'If you are going to give children occasional treats go for homemade energy bars and balls, and ice creams and yoghurts made using non-dairy milks.'

LUNCH

Soup features big in our house. Packed with veg, and with endless combinations to keep it interesting, it's hard to beat. It freezes well and is good with wholegrain bread, or with quinoa, rice or barley left over from dinner added to it to make it a meal.

Some kind of wholemeal bread/cracker/pitta/wrap with any combination of the following: avocado (a staple in our house), hummus, sprouts, chopped cucumber, grated carrot. I don't know what I'd feed the kids if avocados didn't exist! They're delish smeared on toast with tomatoes, olives, hummus, sprouts...again, there are lots of combinations.

DINNER

I'll often cook enough of a meal that I can have an extra dinner in the fridge as well as the one for that night and one to freeze. On days that I'm busy or just can't be bothered, it means I have something healthy and handy to feed us. The times when we eat junky food are when I'm not organized.

Dinner varies hugely for us, from Indian curries to stir-fries and stews. Here are some easy things I do to make sure our dinners are as nutritious as possible:

Use brown rice, wholemeal couscous and brown bread rather than white. This seems obvious, but it makes a massive difference to overall health, especially when you think about how much of this stuff we consume. Also, mix up your grains, using quinoa, barley, wholemeal couscous rather than falling back on rice or spuds all the time.

Use brown pasta (rice or spelt or wholemeal pasta). It actually tastes really good and makes an otherwise stodgy meal healthy.

> 'Put a tiny piece of something you don't expect them
> to like or eat on the plate so it becomes normal for
> them to see it in front of them. '

Substitute regular spuds with sweet potatoes. They provide 400 per cent of your RDA for vitamin A, more fibre and fewer total carbs (despite being slightly higher in sugars). They're great mashed, roasted or oven-baked as chips.

Make one-pot wonders (chilli, stews, curries, pasta sauces, etc.) with small pieces of veg. My girls are pretty good at eating veg generally but they both HATE courgette. They'll eat it when it's chopped into very small pieces in things where it's unidentifiable! It wouldn't be my main method of getting them to eat veg – I generally like them to know what they're eating – but sometimes a bit of trickery gets things into them they wouldn't otherwise touch.

Don't put too much food on their plate. I think kids find it overwhelming to have a mountain of food put in front of them. It represents a challenge or a chore rather than something manageable and enjoyable. I tend to give the kids the full amount of veg I want them to eat on their plate along with a smaller amount of everything else. When they're finished they can go back for more.

Put a tiny piece of something you don't expect them to like or eat on the plate so it becomes normal for them to see it in front of them. The girls have recently started to eat sauerkraut (I'm big into fermented foods) because I'd often put a piece of it on their plate and not make a big deal out of it. For ages they tried and spat it out but eventually their taste-buds changed. Not being forced to eat something makes them far more likely to come to it themselves eventually.

I suppose aside from the practicalities of feeding children healthy food, a lot of what gives them a healthy approach to eating is the feeling around food in the house. Despite our best efforts to hide our issues with food, kids pick up on them. Anxieties around eating too much or too little and poor body image affect our children's ability to have a healthy relationship with food. It's important to make friends with food and find a way of making it something enjoyable. Amidst the chaos of everyday life, sitting down to a meal together can often be the only time in a day where you can actually check in with each other and catch up, and if for no reason other than that, it should be celebrated.

Realistically (for financial reasons as well as time constraints and the need to preserve sanity), every morning can't start with a superfood smoothie and porridge with ten different toppings. And there are times when we eat food on the go that wouldn't be the healthiest fare. But ultimately we do the healthy stuff as much as possible and I try not to beat myself up the other times. A good frozen pizza once in a while never killed anyone!

THE
SWEET
STUFF

GIANT CHOCOLATE PEANUT BUTTER CUP

Our ginormous, super-size take on the classic chocolate peanut butter cup, WAHOO! It is unbelievably straightforward and simple to make and will keep for at least 10 days in your fridge. And it is dairy- and gluten-free!

MAKES 15 SLICES

650g dark chocolate
275g ground almonds
400g peanut butter
    (smooth or chunky; smooth
    is usually used here)
125ml maple syrup
1 tablespoon coconut oil

Using a 23cm shallow springform baking tin with grooves on the sides, line the base and sides with baking parchment, making sure to get it right into all the grooves along the sides of the tin. That will give the finished cake a nice ribbed effect. Fold the foil over the edges.

Melt 350g of the chocolate. Using a pastry brush or a spoon, spread it evenly across the bottom and up the sides of the foil, making sure to cover all the way up the sides. Refrigerate for 20 minutes, until the chocolate hardens.

Put the ground almonds, peanut butter and maple syrup into a large bowl and mix well, using your hands. It will form a nice peanut butter 'dough ball'.

Take the chocolate case out of the fridge, remove from the springform tin and set aside (the parchment will come with it).

Using the base of the springform tin as a template, shape the peanut butter dough into a round even shape the same size. Now you have a filling that's the correct size to fit the chocolate case.

Remove the peanut butter wheel from the base. Put the base back into the springform tin and put the chocolate case back inside. Put the filling into the chocolate case, leaving a little gap around the edge for the dark chocolate topping to marry with the sides of the case.

To make the topping, melt the remaining 300g of dark chocolate, adding the coconut oil (this will make the finished cake easier to cut). Pour the topping over the filling and spread evenly. Use the back of your knife or a long ruler to run over the chocolate and give it a really smooth ripple-free finish. Put into the fridge to set for half an hour.

When set, remove the parchment, cut into slices (using a hot knife), and enjoy!

CHOCOLATE FUDGE CAKE

This is Steve's creation and he is super-proud of it! It is dairy- and egg-free but tastes like it has butter and cream in it. It is totally decadent, a rich chocolate cake with a raspberry coconut cream filling and covered in rich chocolate frosting, one for the true chocoholic!

Preheat your oven to 160°C/325°F/gas mark 3. Line the bases of two 23cm springform cake tins with baking parchment.

Melt the coconut oil and pour into a large bowl. Add all the other cake ingredients and mix with a whisk or a large spoon until the batter is evenly mixed and uniform in texture.

Divide the cake batter evenly between the two tins and bake for 50 minutes in the preheated oven. Test by sticking in a skewer – once the cake is ready, the skewer should come out with some fudge on it and be moist but not wet. It should look like the consistency of a brownie, fudgy and sticky, not thin.

To make the filling, open the tin of coconut milk and remove the fat/cream on top, leaving the watery residue behind. Whisk the coconut cream, maple syrup/agave syrup and vanilla extract together in a bowl until they resemble whipped cream – alternatively you could use an electric whisk. It can take a couple of minutes before you get the desired consistency. Leave in the fridge until your cakes are ready to be dressed.

When your cakes are baked, remove from the oven and leave to cool.

Meanwhile, make the frosting. Melt the chocolate by putting it into a bowl over a pan of hot water. Do not allow the bowl to touch the water. Cut the coconut oil into thin pieces with a knife and add to the melted chocolate. The chocolate will break down the coconut oil. Whisk the chocolate and coconut oil until you get a reasonably solid but malleable paste. This may take up to 15 minutes.

Remove the cooled cakes from their springform tins. Spread the coconut cream on top of one cake and add half the raspberries. Put the other cake on top of the cream-raspberry filling.

MAKES 12–14 SLICES

480ml coconut oil
300g ground almonds
300g white spelt flour/white flour (gluten-free white flour if coeliac)
600ml maple syrup/agave syrup
80g sieved cocoa powder
4 teaspoons baking powder
2 teaspoons salt
480ml rice milk/milk of choice
2 tablespoons vanilla extract

For the filling:
1 x 400ml tin of full-fat coconut milk
1 teaspoon maple syrup/agave syrup
1 tablespoon vanilla extract
125g raspberries

For the frosting:
300g dark chocolate
200g solid coconut oil

Now start to spread the frosting evenly over the top of the cake and down the sides. It's easier if you use a warm knife, spoon or palette knife, so keep a bowl of hot water beside you. Just dry off whatever you are using each time you dip it into the hot water. If the frosting goes too runny, put it into the fridge until it hardens.

Decorate the top with the remaining raspberries. Leave in the fridge for 20 minutes for the chocolate to harden. Scrumptious!

CHOCOLATE PECAN PIES

We wanted to make a healthier version of the classic pecan pie that would still taste epic, so we came up with this vegan version that's raw and full of fibre, and is also rich, nutty, chocolatey, creamy and oh so lovely!

Leave aside 10 pecan nuts to garnish the mini pies.

To make the base, blend the pecan and cashew nuts in a food processor until they reach a rough flour-like consistency. Add the dates, maple syrup and coconut oil and blend the mix until it reaches a uniform consistency. This should only take a couple of minutes.

Put 8 paper cupcake holders into the cups of a muffin tray and divide the base mixture evenly between them. Press and spread it into the cases to get a 1cm base in each. (If you have any extra base left, you can make another little pie!)

To make the filling, put the pecans into the food processor bowl (no need to wash) and whiz until they form a smooth paste, almost like a nut butter. Add the agave or maple syrup and blend for 30 seconds, then add the rest of the ingredients, except the chocolate, and blend until smooth – this will take about 3–4 minutes.

Divide the filling between the mini pies, spreading evenly. If using, grate the chocolate over the pies and put a pecan on each one.

Leave in the fridge for 2 hours to set and harden before serving.

MAKES 8 MINI PIES

For the base:
150g raw pecan nuts
150g raw cashew nuts
100g pitted dates
2 tablespoons maple syrup
2 tablespoons solid coconut oil

For the chocolate pecan
  caramel filling:
150g raw pecan nuts
100ml agave or maple syrup
150g pitted dates
160ml tin of coconut cream/
  cream topping from a 400ml tin
  of full-fat coconut milk
2 tablespoons raw cacao powder
2 tablespoons solid coconut oil
4 squares of dark chocolate
  (optional)

HEALTHIER NO-BAKE CHOCOLATE AND SALTED CARAMEL TART

If you are going to make any cake in this book, this is the one to start with! It's definitely one of our favourite dessert recipes. The salted caramel is made from dates, almond butter and coconut oil, and tastes amazing.

Line the base of a 24cm round non-stick springform cake tin with baking parchment.

To make the base, blend the nuts to a flour-like consistency in a food processor. Add the dates, vanilla extract and coconut oil and whiz again till the mixture resembles breadcrumbs. Press it really firmly into the base of the springform tin, making sure it's evenly spread.

Put all the ingredients for the caramel layer into the same food processor (it should be reasonably clean) and blend till super-smooth and caramel-like. This may take 5–10 minutes – you might need to add a little more water if it is a bit clumpy and isn't blending.

Spread a really even layer of caramel on top of the base layer in the tin, doing your best to give a smooth top ready for the chocolate layer.

Gently melt the chocolate in a heatproof bowl set over a pan of simmering water, making sure the base of the bowl doesn't touch the water. Remove from the heat and pour over the caramel layer. Spread evenly over the caramel.

Put into the fridge and leave to set until the chocolate is solid. Use a hot knife to cut this tart – it will help cut through the chocolate without it cracking.

MAKES 12 SLICES

For the base:
150g walnuts
150g almonds
100g pitted dates
1½ tablespoons vanilla extract
2 tablespoons coconut oil

For the caramel layer:
300g pitted dates
150g almond butter/cashew butter/peanut butter
10–12 tablespoons water
10 tablespoons coconut oil
a large pinch of salt

For the chocolate layer:
300g good-quality dark chocolate (more than 50% solids)

SPRING RHUBARB AND RASPBERRY CRUMBLE

Rhubarb is always one of the first 'fruits' of spring. It's technically a vegetable, but we usually treat it like a fruit. This crumble recipe is dairy-, refined-sugar- and gluten-free (if you use gluten-free oats), so party on! Careful, though – it's so tasty you might end up eating half of it in one sitting! Great served with coconut cream.

Preheat the oven to 160°C/325°F/gas mark 3. We usually make this in a typical household crumble dish/quiche dish (approx. 23cm).

Core the apples and chop into bite-size pieces. Chop the leaves and ends off the rhubarb and cut the stalks into bite-size pieces. Put the apples, rhubarb and raspberries into a medium pot with the honey/maple syrup/agave syrup, cinnamon, ginger and water. Bring to the boil, then reduce to a simmer and cook the fruit for about 20 minutes, or until it has all broken down properly, stirring occasionally. You may need to add a little more water if the fruit is sticking.

If using coconut oil for the crumble, melt it in a pan over a low heat. When melted, pour it (or the sunflower oil) into a bowl and add the oats, ground almonds, pumpkin and sunflower seeds and honey. Stir until really well mixed.

Once the fruit is cooked, pour it into your crumble dish and spread it out evenly. Spread the crumble topping evenly over the fruit and put into the preheated oven for about 20–25 minutes, or until the top of the crumble starts to get nice and golden.

SERVES 6

For the fruit base:
3 medium eating apples
500g rhubarb
125g raspberries
2 tablespoons honey/ maple syrup/
   agave syrup
2 teaspoons ground cinnamon
1 teaspoon ground ginger
4 tablespoons water

For the crumble topping:
5 tablespoons coconut oil/
   sunflower oil
150g oats (use gluten-free
   if you want)
50g ground almonds
3 tablespoons pumpkin seeds
3 tablespoons sunflower seeds
6 tablespoons honey/maple
   syrup/agave syrup

BANOFFEE WITH A TWIST

Our take on the traditional banana and toffee cream pie! Our version needs no baking, it's raw, dairy-, gluten- and refined-sugar-free. and tastes sensational! A nice nutty base is covered with a velvety date caramel, a layer of sliced banana and a silky coconut cream .

Line the base of a 23cm springform cake tin with baking parchment so you can remove the cake easily.

To make the base, put the almonds and cashew nuts into a food processor and whiz until they become coarse crumbs. Add the dates, vanilla extract and coconut oil, and blend until you have a breadcrumb-like texture. Transfer the mixture to the cake tin and use your hands to compact it really firmly into the base, ensuring an even spread.

To make the toffee layer, melt the coconut oil gently in a pan. Put it into a food processor with the rest of the ingredients for the toffee layer and blend until smooth and caramel-like. This can take up to 10 minutes – add more water if it's clumpy. Once ready, spread a really even layer of toffee on top of the base layer, doing your best to give it a smooth top. Put into the fridge for 20 minutes.

The base and toffee layers will keep like this for a week in the fridge, then all you have to do is to dress the cake before you serve. You can have the coconut cream ready in advance too.

Spoon the thick cream from both tins of coconut milk into a mixing bowl. Add 1 tablespoon of the clear coconut milk from one of the tins along with the vanilla extract, and whisk it all together with a fork or an electric whisk. The cream will keep for a week in the fridge, so you can also make this in advance.

To assemble the cake, remove the springform tin, carefully peeling away the parchment lining, and transfer the cake to a flat plate without a dip in it.

Slice the bananas into little 'coins' and put a layer of these on top of the toffee layer. Spoon the coconut cream on top, then, using the fine side of a grater, grate the chocolate on top.

Refrigerate before serving, as the coconut cream will go a bit runny at room temperature if left out for too long. Store the cake in the fridge – if there's any left over!

MAKES 12 SLICES

For the base layer:
100g almonds
300g cashew nuts/walnuts
200g pitted dates
3 teaspoons vanilla extract
4 tablespoons coconut oil

For the toffee layer:
10 tablespoons coconut oil
300g pitted dates
100g tahini (can be replaced with almond butter/cashew butter/peanut butter)
10–12 tablespoons water
1 teaspoon vanilla extract
a pinch of salt (add more if you like it)

For the coconut cream:
2 x 400ml tins of full-fat coconut milk (refrigerated overnight)
1 tablespoon vanilla extract

For the topping:
3 ripe bananas
3 squares of best-quality dark chocolate

LEMON AND LIME AVOCADO MOUSSE CAKE

This is a fresh, zesty and super-smooth raw cake that we have been making for years, and it's always popular. It has a nice balance of sweet and citrus and a lovely crumbly base.

We use 300g of raw nuts in the base – these can be all almonds, cashews, walnuts or pecans, but we usually use a combination of walnuts and almonds. As walnuts can be bitter, we use one-third walnuts and two-thirds almonds. If you want to make this nut-free, use a mix of sunflower and pumpkin seeds.

Line the base of an 18cm springform cake tin with baking parchment.

Put the nuts (or seeds, if you use those) into a food processor and whiz until they turn to coarse crumbs. Add the dates and cacao powder and blend until you reach a breadcrumb-like texture. Add the coconut oil and whiz the mix for a further minute.

Put the mix into the springform tin and spread evenly, compacting it firmly right into the base.

Clean out your food processor. Zest your lime and lemons straight into the processor, then add the juice of the lemons.

Add the avocado flesh, salt, honey/agave syrup and melted coconut oil and whiz again. Check for taste – add more lemon or lime juice or zest, or honey/agave syrup, according to your taste, trying to keep the lovely citrus flavour.

Once you're happy with the taste and texture, spread the topping evenly over the base and refrigerate. The cake will be ready to serve after 2 hours. It will keep for a week in the fridge and freezes well.

SERVES 12

For the base layer:
300g nuts
100g pitted dates
2 tablespoons cacao powder
2 tablespoons melted coconut oil

For the topping:
zest of 1 lime
zest and juice of 2 lemons
3 ripe avocados
a pinch of salt
9 tablespoons honey/agave syrup (135ml)
12 tablespoons melted coconut oil

SUPER FUDGY ALMOND BROWNIES

All-round fab brownies! It's best to deliberately undercook these so that they are really gooey. When you leave them to cool in the fridge afterwards, they harden up and become something in between fudge and brownies!

Preheat the oven to 160°C/325°F/gas mark 3.

Chop the walnuts into small pieces. Leave 50g aside to decorate the brownies.

Melt the coconut oil and pour it into a large bowl. Add all the rest of the ingredients and mix well together until uniform in texture.

Line a flapjack tray (approx. 40cm x 25cm and 3cm high) with baking parchment and pour in the mixture so that it is about 2½cm high.

Bake for 18 minutes in the preheated oven. Once baked, remove from the oven, scatter the chopped walnuts on top and gently press them down so that they are studded in.

Leave to cool at room temperature. When cool, put into the fridge for 30 minutes to set fully and to release its fudge power! Cut into 12 pieces and enjoy!

MAKES 12

150g walnuts
200ml coconut oil
200g ground almonds
100g white spelt flour
300ml maple syrup/agave syrup
40g cocoa powder
2 teaspoons baking powder
1 teaspoon salt
200ml rice milk/milk of
    your choice
1 tablespoon vanilla extract

AMAZING CHOCOLATE, NUT AND CARAMEL BARS

We did a taste test of these in Soho, London, comparing them to the original Snickers™ that inspired them. Guess which won? Our version by 9 to 1! These really taste fab and are fun to make with your kids.

Put all the ingredients for the base into a bowl and mix them together with a fork until they come together into a dough. Roll the dough out into a rectangle about 14cm x 18cm (don't get hung up on exact measures) and ½cm thick, then cut it into 10–15 smaller rectangles, each about 7cm long and 2½cm wide.

Take a baking tray that will fit into your freezer and line it with baking parchment. Put the 'bars' on the baking tray and place in the freezer. Leave to harden for 15 minutes.

In a food processor, blend together all the caramel filling ingredients except the nuts, adding as much water as you need to reach a nice thick paste.

Remove the bar bases from the freezer and spread a thick layer of the date caramel over each one, smoothing the sides with a knife. Sprinkle some chopped nuts on each of the bars, spreading them out evenly. Return the tray to the freezer and leave for another 20–30 minutes.

For the coating, melt the chocolate in a bowl over a pan of simmering water, making sure the base of the bowl doesn't touch the water.

Now it is chocolate covering time! Remove the bars from the freezer. We find the best way to coat the little bars is to put each one on a large knife, hold it over the bowl of melted chocolate, then ladle the chocolate over, covering each one with a lovely velvety layer! One at a time, cover them in the chocolate and put them back on the cold tray. The chocolate will harden almost instantly. Place in the fridge for an hour to firm up fully.

Stored in the fridge, these will keep for about a week.

MAKES ABOUT 10

For the base:
65g agave syrup
240g almond butter
160g ground almonds
a pinch of salt
1 teaspoon vanilla extract

For the caramel filling:
180g pitted dates
90g peanut butter/almond butter
4 tablespoons coconut oil
4–7 teaspoons water
100g chopped roasted almonds
  or peanuts

For the chocolate coating:
300g best-quality dark chocolate
  (70% cocoa solids)

CHOCOLATE COOKIE DOUGH BALLS

Super-tasty little treats, and a great snack to satisfy any sweet cravings! If you want them sugar-free, use cacao nibs instead of dark chocolate. These will keep for about a week in the fridge and can be frozen.

Blend the oats, salt and cashews in a food processor for a couple of minutes, until the mix resembles fine crumbs. Add the dates and blend for a further 2 minutes. Scrape down the sides of the bowl.

Melt the coconut oil and add it to the processor with the vanilla extract. Blend again. You may have to stop your machine and scrape down the sides a number of times to blend properly. If it's too crumbly to form a dough, you can add a couple of teaspoons of water and blend again.

Remove from the processor and put into a large mixing bowl. Add the cacao nibs/dark chocolate chips and fold them in. It should form a big cookie dough ball! Break off pieces and roll them into mini balls (or shape into bars if you'd prefer). Store at room temperature for a few days, or refrigerate or freeze for a few weeks.

MAKES ABOUT 12

30g porridge oats/
   gluten-free oats

a pinch of salt

80g cashews (raw or roasted)

80g chopped dates

2 tablespoons coconut oil

1 teaspoon vanilla extract

3 tablespoons cacao nibs/
   dark chocolate chips

HAPPY PEAR EGG-FREE PAVLOVA

At last – an egg-free meringue! We know this sounds like a total contradiction, and when you see what we are using instead of eggs you will be amazed! This is very straightforward and involves the same steps as a normal pavlova – first you make the meringues and then the cream. The meringues will keep for five days in an airtight container.

Preheat the oven to 110°C/225°F/gas mark ¼.

In a clean bowl, whisk the chickpea liquid for 10 minutes, using an electric hand whisk. It will become thick, stiff and creamy, with soft peaks.

Sprinkle in the caster sugar gradually and keep whisking, adding the sugar into the mixture for a further 5 minutes.

Get out two baking trays. Using the base of a 23cm spring-form tin, draw a circle on a sheet of baking parchment. Draw a second circle beside it. You should be able to draw two circles on each baking tray. Altogether you'll draw four circles.

Spoon the meringue mix to fill your marked circles, then put the two baking trays into the preheated oven for 2½ hours.

When they are ready, take them out, leave to cool for 40 minutes, and carefully peel off the baking parchment.

Skim the cream from the top of each tin of coconut milk. Put into a bowl and add the vanilla extract and 2 tablespoons of the clear coconut milk from the cans. Whisk with an electric whisk for 1 minute to bring it all together and remove any lumps.

Place your base layer of meringue on a flat plate and spread with a layer of coconut cream. Top with fruit of your choice (such as fresh raspberries/strawberries/passion fruit/kiwi/mango). Repeat until you are left with a last layer of meringue to put on top, then finish with some coconut cream, and decorate with fruit and mint leaves. Enjoy!

SERVES 4–6

liquid from 1 x 400g tin
    of chickpeas
125g caster sugar

To layer and top your pavlova:
4 x 400ml tins of
    full-fat coconut milk
    (refrigerated overnight)
2 teaspoons vanilla extract
300g soft fruit of your choice
a few mint leaves

VEGAN KNICKERBOCKER GLORY

This is our dairy- and gluten-free take on the famous layered cream sundae. The meringue part of this recipe is time-consuming to make simply for this recipe, so it might be best to make a pavlova and use one of your meringues to crumble through these delights. Big sundae glasses and long spoons are essential to make this dessert shine!

It is really just a matter of layering it all up as in the photograph – we usually put raspberries on the bottom, then a scoop of ice-cream, then dark chocolate chips, another scoop of ice-cream, then fruit of our choice (passion fruit and mandarins are great). We top things off with coconut cream and finally garnish with raspberries, grated chocolate and some mint leaves!

SERVES 4

125g raspberries
2 passion fruits
  (flesh scooped out)
2 mandarin oranges,
  segmented (see page 96)
50g dark chocolate chips
½ a portion of meringue recipe
  (see page 216)
½ a portion of an ice-cream
  recipe (see pages 220–21)
½ a portion of coconut cream
  (see page 253)

To garnish:
some grated chocolate
a few mint leaves

DAIRY-FREE ICE-CREAM FOUR WAYS

Delicious and creamy, just like the full-fat and sugary stuff that we all love. We use coconut milk and cashews to give a smooth texture, and sweeten with agave syrup or maple syrup. Each of these only takes five minutes to make and then it's just a matter of freezing. If you have an ice-cream maker this will help make it creamier and smoother, but it is not essential.

VANILLA ICE-CREAM

MAKES 600ML

400ml full-fat coconut milk
100g roasted cashew nuts
1 tablespoon vanilla extract or
    the seeds from ½ a vanilla pod
100g agave syrup

Whiz all the ingredients in a blender until smooth. Pour into a plastic container with a lid and freeze for 6 hours. If you have an ice-cream machine this will make it lighter and fluffier.

CHOCOLATE CHIP COOKIE DOUGH ICE-CREAM

MAKES 700ML

1 batch of chocolate chip cookie
    dough (see page 215)
1 batch of vanilla ice-cream
    (see above)

Form the cookie dough into little bite-size balls.

You can either make a fresh batch of vanilla ice-cream from the recipe above and pour it into two flat plastic storage containers, or, if you have a batch of vanilla ice-cream already made, simply thaw it until it softens.

Add the cookie dough balls and mix them through. Put the lids on the containers and freeze for about 4–6 hours.

MINT CHOCOLATE CHIP ICE-CREAM

MAKES 600ML

400ml full-fat coconut milk
100g raw cashew nuts
100ml almond milk/milk
  of your choice
100g agave syrup
1 teaspoon spirulina
5 drops of peppermint oil
100g dark chocolate chips

Really tasty stuff! The spirulina gives it its green colour and the drops of peppermint oil give it a real mint kick. A total winner. If you like a really minty flavour, add more peppermint oil, and do likewise if you like more choc chips!

Whiz all the ingredients in a food processor, leaving out the choc chips.

Once blended, pour into a plastic container. Fold in the dark chocolate chips, then put the lid on and put into the freezer for 4–6 hours. Don't worry if all the chips sink to the bottom of the mix when you add them. Just freeze for an hour, then take out the container, stir them through and freeze again.

OLIVE OIL, HONEY AND COCONUT ICE-CREAM

MAKES 900ML

1 x 400ml tin of full-fat
  coconut milk
150g cashew nuts
6 tablespoons honey
  (you can use agave syrup
  to make this vegan)
250ml olive oil

Our head chef, Juan, is Spanish and loves olive oil, so this is one of his favourite ice-creams. The flavour may sound a little strange, but believe us, it is super-tasty . . . it will leave people wondering, 'What is it I'm tasting?'

Put all the ingredients into a blender and whiz until smooth.

Put into a plastic container with a lid and freeze for about 4–6 hours.

SUPERFOOD FUDGE

Superfood and fudge in the same sentence . . . how does that work? Well, this is a fudge that is gluten-, dairy- and refined-sugar-free, requires no cooking or baking, tastes fab and even contains superfoods! Makes great guilt-free edible presents too!

Melt the coconut oil gently over a low heat. Pour it into a mixing bowl and add all the remaining ingredients, keeping back 1 tablespoon each of goji berries and cacao nibs. Mix really well until smooth and silky.

Pour into a 500ml plastic storage container with high sides, so that the fudge is approx 2½cm high. Top with the remaining tablespoon of goji berries and cacao nibs.

Put on the lid and refrigerate for 4 hours. When ready, cut up and enjoy!

FILLS A 500ML CONTAINER

6 tablespoons coconut oil
200g almond butter
120g honey/maple syrup/agave syrup/date syrup
1 teaspoon vanilla extract
a pinch of sea salt
2 tablespoons raw cacao powder
4 tablespoons goji berries
4 tablespoons raw cacao nibs
60g ground almonds

POMEGRANATE AND PISTACHIO HALVA

Halva is a tasty **Middle Eastern treat made with sesame seed paste (tahini) and honey.
Our version takes ten minutes to make and will keep for at least two weeks in the fridge.
It also freezes really well and makes a great gift.**

Melt the coconut oil gently over a low heat.

Pour the melted coconut oil, tahini, honey and ground almonds into a large mixing bowl, then add the vanilla extract and salt and mix thoroughly with a fork.

Cut the pomegranate in half. Put one half face down on a chopping board and bang the back until the seeds fall out. Repeat with the other half. Drain any extra juice from the seeds and remove any white pith. Finely chop the pistachios/cashews.

Stir half the pomegranate seeds and half the chopped pistachios/cashews through the mixture, keeping the rest to decorate the top.

Pour the mixture into a 500ml plastic storage container with a lid. Top with the remaining pistachios/cashews and pomegranate seeds, and put into the fridge for a few hours, until set.

FILLS A 500ML CONTAINER

4 tablespoons coconut oil
280g tahini
120g honey/agave syrup
60g ground almonds
1 teaspoon vanilla extract
a small pinch of salt
1 pomegranate
4 tablespoons pistachio nuts/
  cashew nuts

SUPERFOOD ENERGY BALLS THREE WAYS

These take just ten minutes to make and are great for children and adults alike! They are a great quick and filling snack, with the added benefit of three different flavours. If you don't have the ingredients for one type, just make more of the others.

Put the cashew nuts, dates and salt into a food processor and blend till quite smooth.

Gently heat the coconut oil until melted, add to the processor together with the water, and blend again.

Divide the mixture between three bowls. To the first of the bowls, add the ingredients for the green mint balls and mix by hand until the mixture becomes one solid colour (less than a minute). Roll into 4 or 5 balls.

Add the ingredients for the mocha balls to the second bowl and mix by hand until the mixture comes together into a uniform dark brown colour. Roll into 4 or 5 balls.

To make the superfood balls, finely chop the goji berries and mix with the bee pollen. Roll the last third of the mixture into 4 or 5 balls and roll them in the goji-pollen mixture to get a nice colourful coating.

MAKES 12–15

For the base:
100g cashew nuts
100g chopped dates
a pinch of salt
3 tablespoons coconut oil
1 teaspoon water

For the green mint balls:
¼ teaspoon spirulina
2 drops of mint oil

For the mocha balls:
1 teaspoon ground coffee
1 teaspoon cocoa powder

For the superfood balls:
1 tablespoon goji berries
1 tablespoon bee pollen

SUPERFOOD BALLS   GREEN MINT BALLS   MOCHA BALLS

SUPERFOOD ENERGY BALLS THREE WAYS

CHOCOLATE TRUFFLES WITH BEE POLLEN

CHOCOLATE TRUFFLES WITH GOJI BERRIES

CHOCOLATE TRUFFLES WITH CHOPPED PISTACHIOS

CHOCOLATE TRUFFLES THREE WAYS

These decadent, silky chocolate truffles make a wonderful gift. They are really easy to make and so worth the effort.

Gently heat the coconut oil until melted. Put the rest of the base ingredients into a mixing bowl that will fit into your freezer, then add the melted coconut oil and mix really well. Put into the freezer for 15 minutes, until the mixture sets and becomes firm.

Roll the mixture into balls, making sure you don't handle them too much or they will melt. This amount should make about 24 small truffles (about 2cm in diameter – half the size of a golfball).

Finely chop the goji berries and the pistachio nuts separately. Lay them out on separate small plates, putting the bee pollen on a third plate.

Divide your balls into three batches. Roll each batch of balls in a different coating – goji berries, pistachios and bee pollen. This will give you three types of fab-looking chocolate truffles.

Store in the fridge in a container for up to 10 days. Enjoy!

MAKES 24

For the truffle base:
85g coconut oil
60g ground almonds
40g cocoa powder
120g honey/agave syrup
½ teaspoon sea salt
1 tablespoon vanilla extract

For coating:
4 tablespoons goji berries
4 tablespoons chopped
   pistachios
4 tablespoons bee pollen

ENERGY BALLS

Steve's son, Theo, is officially the energy ball monster! He loves them, and Steve is happy for him to eat a few at a go, as they are nutritious and full of fibre – the perfect healthy treat! Also, being nut-free, we give them to our kids as a snack in their lunchbox for school.

Chop the dates into small pieces and soak in the apple juice/orange juice for a few minutes.

Pulse the oats and sunflower seeds in a food processor for 30 seconds. Add the soaked dates and the juice together with the raisins and cocoa powder. Add the zest of 1 orange. Alternatively, you could use mint oil or ground coffee to give a different flavour.

Blend all the ingredients until the mix has a smooth texture, which could take up to 2 minutes.

Roll into small balls (about the size of a small Brussels sprout) and roll in the coating of your choice. We generally use desiccated coconut, but you could use bee pollen to give a yellow coating or chopped goji berries for red.

MAKES ABOUT 40 X 15G BALLS

170g pitted dates
125ml apple juice/orange juice
100g porridge oats
60g sunflower seeds
60g raisins
2 tablespoons cocoa powder
zest of 1 orange/3 teaspoons mint oil/2 teaspoons ground coffee
50g desiccated coconut/bee pollen/goji berries

PROTEIN BARS

Mighty little bars – very filling. We use pea protein, but use whatever you have; it is not even essential, as this recipe is packed full of energy-rich seeds. A nice one for lunchboxes.

Put the dates into a bowl and cover them with boiling water. You could also soak them in hot mint tea if you like, to add another depth of flavour.

Pulse all the dry ingredients in a food processor for about 30 seconds. You still want a bit of bite to them. Place the dry mixture in a bowl and set aside.

Drain the dates, then put into the food processor together with the rest of the wet ingredients and mix until smooth. This might take some time, and you may have to scrape down the sides and/or add a few tablespoons of water. It should be the texture of sticky dark caramel.

Pour the wet ingredients into the bowl of dry ingredients and stir until well combined.

Spread the mix evenly in a 30cm x 18cm flapjack tray lined with baking parchment and place in the fridge for 30 minutes. Then cut into bars and store in an airtight container.

MAKES 12

The dry ingredients:
120g pumpkin seeds
50g desiccated coconut
50g sesame seeds
80g ground flax seeds
  (see page 252)
50g protein powder
40g chia seeds
45g goji berries

The wet ingredients:
250g pitted dates
140g melted coconut oil
75ml honey/maple syrup/
  agave syrup
4 tablespoons cacao powder
1 teaspoon vanilla extract

NEW-TELLA

A healthier chocolate spread: sounds like a dream, doesn't it? Great with pancakes or on toast, and tasty enough to eat straight off a spoon!

Preheat the oven to 170°C/325°F/gas mark 3.

First make your hazelnut butter. Roast the hazelnuts on a baking sheet in the preheated oven for 8 minutes, until they are nicely roasted, with their skins loose, darker brown and smelling fab.

Put the roasted hazelnuts into a food processor with the sunflower oil and salt and blend until the mix becomes nice, smooth and runny. In some food processors it will be done in 5 minutes and in others it may take up to 15 minutes. You will need to scrape down the sides a few times. (Alternatively you can simply use a jar of roasted hazelnut butter and save this step! It's available in many health food stores.)

Once your roasted hazelnut butter is ready, transfer it from the food processor into a mixing bowl and add all the rest of the ingredients. Mix together well with a fork.

Put it into a sterilized jar, where it will keep for a month at room temperature. Enjoy!

MAKES 450G

330g hazelnuts
2 tablespoons sunflower oil
a pinch of sea salt
80ml honey/maple syrup/agave syrup
2 tablespoons cacao powder
1 teaspoon vanilla extract

HOMEMADE CORDIALS FOUR WAYS

These go wonderfully well with some sparkling water on a summer's evening. Served in a wine glass with some berries in the bottom, they form a gorgeous alcohol-free cocktail. These cordials work best using one part cordial to six parts water, but you can adjust the proportions to your taste.

LEMONGRASS AND LEMON CORDIAL

4 stalks of lemongrass
2 lemons (ideally unwaxed)
250g agave syrup/maple syrup
250ml water

The lemongrass adds a lovely floral undertone to this zesty cordial.

Roughly chop the lemongrass and put it into a large saucepan. Zest the lemons into the pan, then slice the lemons and add them to the pan too.

Add the agave syrup and water and slowly bring to the boil, stirring occasionally to mix. Once it boils, lower the temperature and let it simmer gently for around 20 minutes.

Take off the heat, leave to cool for 15 minutes, then pour into a bowl through a fine sieve or a sieve lined with muslin. Transfer into sterilized bottles (see page 259 on how to sterilize bottles and jars), using a funnel.

Once cool, store in the fridge. This will keep for 3–4 weeks.

STRAWBERRY AND RASPBERRY CORDIAL

500g strawberries
125g raspberries
250g agave syrup
3 cloves
250ml water

Stephen's favourite! There is a strong flavour of stewed strawberry, with the slightly more acid raspberry in the background – lovely with sparkling water!

Remove the stems from the strawberries and roughly chop with the raspberries. Put into a large saucepan.

Add the agave syrup and cloves, along with the water, and slowly bring to the boil over a medium heat, stirring occasionally to mix. Once it comes to the boil, lower the temperature and let it simmer gently for around 20 minutes.

Take off the heat and leave to cool for 15 minutes, then pour into a bowl or jug through a fine sieve or a sieve lined with muslin. Transfer into sterilized bottles (see page 259 on how to sterilize bottles and jars), using a funnel.

Once cool, store in the fridge. Keeps for 3–4 weeks.

ORANGE, CARDAMOM AND GINGER CORDIAL

4 medium oranges
150g fresh ginger
6 cardamom pods
250g agave syrup
250ml water

Aromatic and fragrant, with a strong sweet citrus flavour. We love the ginger in this, as it grounds the orange flavour, giving a lovely balanced feel to this drink.

Slice the unpeeled oranges and ginger into a large saucepan. Add the cardamom pods.

Add the agave syrup to the pan, along with the water, and slowly bring to the boil, stirring occasionally to mix. Once it comes to the boil, lower the temperature and let it simmer gently for around 20 minutes.

Take off the heat, leave to cool for 15 minutes, then pour into a bowl or jug through a fine sieve or a sieve lined with muslin. Transfer into sterilized bottles (see page 259 on how to sterilize bottles and jars), using a funnel.

Once cool, store in the fridge. Keeps for 3–4 weeks.

FROM LEFT TO RIGHT: ELDERFLOWER CORDIAL | ORANGE, CARDAMOM AND GINGER CORDIAL | STRAWBERRY AND RASPBERRY CORDIAL | LEMONGRASS AND LEMON CORDIAL

ELDERFLOWER CORDIAL

10 large heads of elderflower
250ml boiling water
1 lemon
1 orange
450ml honey/agave syrup
a thumb-size piece of
    fresh ginger

If you are lucky enough to have some elder bushes growing in your own or a friend's garden, or can get out into the countryside, elderflowers are well worth harvesting for this wonderfully classy floral drink. It goes down so well on a summer's afternoon with some sparkling water. We also serve it with prosecco in our evening restaurant.

You need to be careful when selecting your flowers – they are only at their best for about three weeks in June (in Ireland). The heads should be white, not cream or with any brown flowers, and they should not fall too readily when shaken. The main crop is the most fragrant. It must be a dry day when you pick, otherwise rogue yeasts develop. The blooms should smell lemony.

Pick off any insects you see on the elderflowers. Use the back of a fork to remove the flowers from the stalks into a large bowl.

Pour the boiling water into the bowl. Zest the lemon on top, then squeeze in the juice from the lemon and the orange, making sure not to let any pips get in. Add the sliced ginger.

Leave to cool down for about 5 minutes, then add the honey/agave syrup, mix well and leave to brew overnight.

In the morning, pour into a bowl or jug through a sieve lined with a muslin cloth. Transfer into sterilized bottles (see page 259 on how to sterilize bottles and jars), using a funnel. This should keep for about a month in the fridge.

Before serving, dilute the elderflower 1:4 with sparkling or still water. Adding a few blueberries and raspberries to the glass before serving will give it a classy look!

OUR COFFEE OBSESSION

When we first opened our café we were so idealistic that we didn't want to sell coffee at all, as we thought it was an addictive stimulant! Thankfully people convinced us otherwise, but our enthusiasm for coffee was non-existent – it was just something we had to sell because it was expected in a café. It wasn't until our childhood friend Paul Grimes came to work with us that we saw the light! Paul (aka Paulie G/PG/'the chief') has an infectious passion for good coffee and has managed to turn two health-obsessive coffee-haters into complete enthusiasts.

Speciality coffee is a relatively new thing. A few years ago we were completely unaware of the wonderful underground world of coffee obsession and general geekiness around all things coffee – roasting, extracting, brewing and serving a cup of coffee being carried out with as much care and detail as performing brain surgery! (A cup of coffee in Paul's house is like a science experiment, and it can take anything from an hour to a week to get the perfect brew on the table, but he says it's always worth the wait.)

Paul inspired Steve to compete in the Irish Barista Championships in 2014 on four weeks' notice. Never short of confidence, Steve was convinced he would win and had informed his friend in Seattle, where the world championships were being held, that he was coming to visit! Steve didn't win but gave it his all and had a laugh. He did manage to win the Vice Dublin Latté Art Throw-down, where passionate baristas go head-to-head in front of a crowd to pour their prettiest design on the top of a cup of coffee. There is a real art to pouring a perfect tulip or rosette and it's a way for a barista to turn what could be a mundane task into a form of artistic expression.

With the arrival of PG, a wave of coffee-loving staff joined our team, including Shane and Raj. These became the backbone of our 'bro-ista' team (which includes a few sisters) and the secret society of the CPA (coffee perverts' association!). A real buzz around coffee emerged in the Happy Pear. We regularly host in-house latté art throw-downs which give our baristas a chance to show off, share their latest techniques, have a laugh and drink some beers.

We still claim that we don't drink coffee, but we absolutely love to taste it and to try different espressos when we're travelling. We especially love the art and care that goes into good coffee. We have found that coffee has been a real connector. The old idea that it's not what you do, but how you do it, that counts really rings true for us. We regularly go on coffee research tours around Europe with the CPA to meet and learn from other enthusiasts and to be inspired by our shared coffee passion!

Right from the start of the Happy Pear we were all about the natural artisanal approach, so inevitably we felt drawn to one day roasting our own coffee – not for commercial reasons, but the idea of learning an old food art really appealed to us. Once Paul and Shane were on board, it was just a matter of doing it. As ever, we went into the unknown head-first with nothing but passion and a blind faith that things would work out. We visited many roasteries and renowned coffee shops around Europe and North America to learn secret ninja roasting skills, and with the help of some actual solid roasting training we managed to turn a dream into a reality and we now roast all our own speciality coffee.

"A few years ago we were completely unaware of the wonderful underground world of coffee obsession and general geekiness around all things coffee – roasting, extracting, brewing and serving a cup of coffee being carried out with as much care and detail as performing brain surgery!"

HERE ARE OUR TEAM'S TOP TIPS FOR BREWING THE PERFECT CUP OF JOE AT HOME

We serve our very best lattés, flat whites and espressos from our big shiny expensive espresso machines. Even though George Clooney and home espresso machine manufacturers would like you to believe it, small home espresso machines can't do the same job, otherwise we would be using them in our cafés.

Amazingly, it is possible to make fantastic brewed coffee in your PJs, from the comfort of your own home, that will match some of the best filter coffee from any high end café around the world, and for very little expense. There is no need for expensive gear. All you need is:

- A GOOD GRINDER. Inexpensive hand grinders are perfect (e.g. Hario or Porlex) or an electric burr grinder. Cheap grinders make terrible coffee!
- A GOOD BREWING DEVICE. A pour-over brewer (e.g. V60 or Chemex), or an immersion brewer such as a French press (aka cafetière) or a Clever Dripper.
- FRESHLY ROASTED COFFEE BEANS (Happy Pear, of course!). Find your local quality focused roaster or find great roasters online.
- A CHEAP DIGITAL WEIGHING SCALES (should cost less than 25 euros).
- FRESH FILTERED OR BOTTLED WATER (tap water is not a great choice).
- A KETTLE

Use the scales to weigh out your coffee and water. The idea behind weighing everything is that if you make a lovely-tasting coffee, once you know your measurements you'll be able to repeat it. A good ratio to use would be 60g/litre – that's 60g of coffee to 1 litre of water. A litre is a lot of coffee, so if you were brewing enough for one person you might use something like 18g of coffee to 300ml of water.

Use fresh filtered or bottled water when it's just off the boil. Or if you really want to geek out, and dive into the science and craft of brewing really great coffee at home, buy a small thermometer and experiment to discover the optimal temperature of the water to get the best coffee. Geek out if you must, but make sure you have fun with it!

We always roast, serve and drink light to medium roasted coffee. We find this is the best way to taste the natural flavour of the coffee and not roasty burnt flavours.

TIPS FOR BUYING GOOD BEANS

- Try to buy online from a good speciality roaster (like us) or your local quality coffee house (a coffee house that cares!).
- Ensure there is a roast date on the bag and always use within eight weeks max, whether you've opened it or not.

'We visited many roasteries and renowned coffee shops and with some solid training we turned a dream into a reality and we now roast our own coffee.'

FLYNNERS' FRUIT & VEG FOR SOCIAL CHANGE

'We are both very idealistic, and values and ethics are intertwined into the fabric of our business.'

Recently Dave came across a list of names we were considering when we started the business. One of main alternatives to the Happy Pear was 'Flynners' Fruit & Veg for Social Change'! Catchy, eh? Though we laugh about it, the name captures what we were all about when we started out. In fact, we Flynners are still all about 'fruit and veg for social change'.

Because we started the Happy Pear with a vision of making the world a happier and healthier place, it has given us a focus and something to underpin all our efforts and decisions. It has made working long hours and doing the routine repetitive stuff easier. We know we're building something we believe in.

The Happy Pear is really an extension of our values, and underlying everything we do is a way of living that gives our lives more meaning than the western promise of fulfilment through money, possessions and material achievement. The Happy Pear is the vehicle we use to share this message!

In the early days Steve was in the Dublin Fruit Market on a summer's morning at 4.30 a.m. and ran into an old college friend, Alan Coleman, who was still out partying from the night before. Alan was in great spirits and looking to kill time before the first train home, so he

was delighted to join in the morning's trading. Alan had such fun that he came out to the shop with Steve. He ended up staying most of the morning, stocking the shop, meeting people and having a laugh. After this he decided he would come work with us and 'play shop'. He worked with us for a couple of years and was a great asset. 'The Happy Pear doesn't just do healthy food,' Alan said once. 'Life is tough out there and it's hard work and the Happy Pear is like a balm to modern life – a soul massage!' We like that!

We are both very idealistic, and values and ethics are intertwined into the fabric of our business. However, every day they get constantly challenged. What is ethically sound doesn't always make the best commercial sense. But having ideals has made decision-making easier. It's like having a tuning fork: we know immediately if something chimes with our vision or not. Not only does a decision feel right; but we can rationalize it.

Recently we had to choose between using compostable or regular recyclable takeaway coffee cups. The compostable cup was made of vegetable-based starches and the recyclable cup had a plastic lining made of petrochemicals. The compostable cup would cost an extra €7,000 per year. We chose the compostable cup because it's better for the environment. It was a no-brainer. For a similar reason we gave up selling bottled water about five years ago: it just wasn't a fit with our values. We didn't want to contribute more plastic to the environment so we put a good filter on our water fountains.

From the beginning, our hope was that the Happy Pear vision for a happier healthier world would inspire others to join in. Today, the thriving Happy Pear community shows that it makes sense to a lot of people. Many people who start out as customers share a similar vision and try to make changes in their own lives. In our experience, finding and building a community of like-minded people is where it is at; people are inspired by a collective dream of making things better.

We have found customers to be very understanding of the chaos that idealism can bring! At lunchtime and at weekends there are sometimes long queues at the café. People seem to appreciate the cheerful personal touch rather than robotic efficiency (though we do try to be efficient!). Last year we put our heads together to work out how to turn the queuing into a more meaningful experience. We started to do tastings with those in the queue – our pestos, whatever fruit is in season, some of our sweet treats. It's a

'From the beginning, our hope was that the Happy Pear vision for a happier healthier world would inspire others to join in.'

'Our granny used to say that our motto was "Be happy, have fun!" Granny was right: for us it really is that simple!'

way of engaging with people and thanking them for coming and being patient. From a business point of view, it doesn't make sense to give away stuff, but it creates a lovely fun atmosphere and that is more important to us than watching every cent.

This chapter is all about how we do business and sharing our experiences so that, hope-fully, we can inspire you. But there is one thing that's special to us that most people won't be able to replicate – having a twin as a business partner! We say that while some people are room-mates we were 'womb-mates' – corny but true! Not only that, but being identical twins, we started as a single egg. As a result we have had a very special relationship right from the start. Hopefully what comes to us naturally – a shared vision, fun, unwavering support of each other – is something you can cultivate in any project you are working on. Our granny used to say that our motto was 'Be happy, have fun!' Granny was right: for us it really is that simple!

Being playful doesn't mean being frivolous. If anything we are more driven. Whereas normally 1 + 1 = 2, in our case, with both of us being very passionate, thinking along the same lines and having the same goals and dreams, there is a multiplier effect and 1 + 1 can equal 3 or more. We drive each other on and get the best out of each other.

On the negative side, our weaknesses and blind spots are compounded by the 1 + 1 = 3 effect! Over the years we have learned that we are good at the big picture stuff – dreaming, ideals and getting things started. We love being in our happy twin bubble planning shiny new projects, and are much less interested in systems, structures, procedures and general business controls and order.

Because work is fun for us, the concept of 'work-life balance' is something we have never been into or believed in. The idea that life is for your hobbies, family and pleasure, and work is an obligation rather than something that's a source of creativity, challenge and joy doesn't make sense to us. (Having said that, we each have two small children and we struggle with balancing work and family life. A number of times when Steve has come back from a week's holiday, his wife, Justyna, has said that she hadn't seen him so excited since before they left. And every day when one of us is on holiday he is calling the other one to check in on what he is missing!)

It's a constant juggling act, getting the balance right between being so many different things: being commercial and also being true to our goals and dreams; having systems but still leaving enough autonomy for our team; having enough structure that it supports rather than stifles; getting prices right so they aren't too high or too low. This constant battle has given us a wonderful capacity to thrive and feel very much at home in chaos!

Back when we started the shop Steve was adamant that we set up our business as a charity, as he wanted it to be explicit that we were not in this for profit but to create a better world. Thankfully Dad talked us round and so we set up the Happy Pear as a regular business. However, money was still a dirty word for us and as a result, during the first few years, we had little focus on costs or sales. Our accountant did our annual return but we took no interest in the numbers side of the business. Instead we were into having a good time, bringing people together and spreading our message (eat more veg!). About four years after we started, one of our investors threatened to bring someone in to manage things, as they didn't think we were fit to run a business. It was a bit of a wake-up call!

It has taken us about ten years to make peace with the idea of money and profit. We are both dreamers, and fulfilling big dreams usually requires big resources. Nowadays any profit is simply a means to fuel growth and to help make our dreams real.

So we have learned that we can't be rigid in our idealism. It has to grow and develop. A couple of events that we have been a part of in the last year have challenged our ideals. At a street food festival in Carnaby Street in London we hosted an event where seven other chefs were cooking, and most of their dishes were meat-based. We had to talk about their dishes and pass samples out to the crowd. Given that we're veg men, that felt totally weird. And still it felt like the right thing to do – helping to celebrate the food that these great chefs believed in. And when Steve was judging a cheffing competition, virtually all the dishes the young chefs produced centred on meat. He didn't taste anything, instead he judged the contestants on their approach to cooking their dish, on their presence, and who he would hire!

At a recent staff barbecue we didn't want to insist that it be veg only. So all the veg were roasted first, and anyone who wanted meat cooked it then. It was a BYOM – Bring Your Own Meat – party!

We find business to be the most fun game we have played and see it as a tremendous tool for having a positive impact on society. We have many dreams and visions of a happier and healthier world and are super-excited about the adventures ahead!

'We love being in our happy twin bubble planning shiny new projects, and are much less interested in systems, structures, procedures and general business controls and order.'

TOP TIPS AND A FEW OF OUR FAVOURITE THINGS

Some of the ingredients we use you might not be familiar with, so this is our glossary of the more exotic wild and wonderful things we use. We have also included notes on some more common ingredients that deserve their moment in the spotlight. You will find these in most health food or Asian shops, and good supermarkets. We're confident that everything we use is available out there, so you won't come across something here that you simply cannot find. We have also included some housekeeping tips.

BARLEY

Barley is a wonderfully versatile grain with a rich nutlike flavour and an appealing chewy consistency. It is deeply nourishing and so soothing on cold winter days! It was widely eaten in Ireland before rice took over. It is usually available as pearl barley (the refined white version of the grain) or as pot barley (the brown wholegrain version). Pot barley is the one we use, but pearl is usually used in barley risottos. It is loaded with fibre and is super-soothing for our digestion. It's great for blood flow and it warms the cockles of your heart. Contains gluten.

BEE POLLEN

One of Dave and his daughters' favourite superfoods. They eat it most days – in smoothies, on top of porridge, straight off a spoon! It is usually a mixture of pollen (the male seed of flowers, e.g. the yellow dusty stuff in the centre of lilies and other flowers that stains your clothes), honey and bee saliva. It is the food of the young bee and is about 40 per cent protein. It is heralded as one of the most complete foods on the planet, containing all the nutrients required by humans. Hippocrates, the father of modern medicine, is reputed to have prescribed it to people who were malnourished in Ancient Greece.

One of the most interesting facts about bee pollen is that it cannot be synthesized in a laboratory. When researchers take away a bee's pollen-filled comb and feed it the man-made pollen, the bee dies even though all the pollen's

known nutrients are present in the lab version. Despite thousands of studies of bee pollen it appears that it contains something that the scientists just can't identify – a mysterious 'B-factor' that could explain why it works so brilliantly!

BUCKWHEAT FLOUR

Although it sounds like it must be part of the wheat family, buckwheat is a seed and is gluten-free. It is a whole-food flour with a nice sweet flavour and a dense texture. We use it lots in pancakes.

"BEE POLLEN: heralded as one of the most complete foods on the planet, containing all the nutrients required by humans. Hippocrates, the father of modern medicine, is reputed to have prescribed it to people who were malnourished in Ancient Greece.

One of the most interesting facts about bee pollen is that it cannot be synthesized in a laboratory."

CELERIAC

A great root veg that's starchy like a potato and has a mild flavour of celery. We use lots of this in our soups. It usually requires peeling.

CHIA AND FLAX SEEDS*

We classify both these seeds as total superfoods primarily for their high levels of omega-3 fatty acids. Both are also very high in fibre and protein (they have protein levels similar to meat). Flax contains more protein but chia seeds contain all nine essential amino acids, making them a complete protein, while flax is missing a couple. While both are great to include in your diet, if you had to pick one, flax seeds have a thick husk that cannot be digested, so they must be ground for your body to get at the nutrients. (They are difficult to chew, so if they're not ground they pass right through your gut and out the other end in the same state they went in!) Chia can be eaten whole or ground, making chia slightly more versatile.

*Flax seed is the American name. In Europe the name linseed is more commonly used. However, the two words are becoming more interchangeable in Europe and we tend to call them flax seeds.

CARDAMOM

Cardamom has a distinctive spicy-sweet taste, more aromatic than spicy. It is usually available in a pod or ground. Ground cardamom can be quite flavourless and you will get more flavour from pods. It is a little more expensive than most spices. Originally from India, it is used in different ways by different cultures: in the Middle East to flavour coffee, in Scandinavia as a baking spice, in India as a savoury spice for curries. We use it in both savoury and sweet dishes.

CHILLI FLAKES

These are fairly easy to find now. They are dried and crushed red chillies that have been flaked and often include lots of seeds. They're great if you like a bit of spice and can be added to just about any dish.

COCONUT CREAM

This works brill as a dairy-free vegan cream. It is the solid fat part at the top of a tin of coconut milk. You simply open the tin, pour off the watery liquid, and whip up the thick creamy white fat that's left with a little vanilla extract. More of the fat turns solid if you refrigerate the tin for a few hours, so if you have time you will get more cream by doing this.

COCONUT CREAM CONCENTRATE

This is made in a similar way to nut butter, with all the coconut flesh being blended to a soft creamy consistency. It's available in jars and also in handy block form. It has high levels of coconut oil but is not the same thing. If it's very cold, leave it out at room temperature to soften slightly so it's easier to use.

DATES

We use plenty of dates in our baking. They are great to sweeten bars, for bases of cakes and in smoothies. Medjool are the fancy dates that are usually more moist and succulent. But we generally just use regular dates (stones removed), and usually soak them in warm water before using.

EDAMAME BEANS

AKA soya beans! These beautiful bright green emeralds add fab colour and a sense of vitality to any dish – they are worth seeking out and are great to have in the freezer. When fresh they come in pods like peas, but we very rarely come by them fresh in Ireland. In the Happy Pear we get them frozen, as they still have their vibrant green colour. They are available in tins but they look brownish rather than bright green, so frozen are better. Replace with frozen peas if you can't source them.

'FLAX EGGS'

This is a handy egg substitute using ground flax seeds. It's better to grind the seeds yourself rather than buy already milled seeds. Simply grind some flax seeds (or chia seeds) in a coffee grinder or high-speed blender. For each egg, combine 1 tablespoon of ground flax seed (measured after grinding) with 3 tablespoons of water, stir well and leave sit for 10 minutes to thicken. After 10 minutes the result should be a sticky, egg-like consistency.

MISO PASTE

Miso paste is made from fermented soya beans and barley or rice. It is central to Japanese cookery and is usually aged anywhere from 6 to 36 months. It gives dishes that meaty umami taste. It's great in sauces, salad dressings and marinades. We haven't got around to making our own miso paste yet, but it's on the list!

NUTRITIONAL YEAST

AKA hippie dust! We first came across nutritional yeast when we hitched across the States visiting organic farms and intentional communities, and loads of people referred to it as 'hippie dust' because all the vegans and veggies loved to sprinkle it on their food! It adds a lovely cheesy flavour without the fat. It's also a great source of vitamin B12 and beneficial bacteria – something to watch if you are a vegan. It's great added to stews, chillies and soups, adding instant flavour.

OIL

Vegetable oils in their many forms – whether cold pressed organic coconut oil or local rapeseed oil or even 'heart healthy' extra virgin olive oil – are all refined foods that are almost 100 per cent fat and have no fibre. So in essence they are empty calories that don't fill you up and add extra calories. As humans we are hardwired to love fat (because it has twice the calories of protein or carbohydrate), but if you are being particularly careful about your health you can get all your fats very easily from eating whole foods rather than refined oil. And if you have high cholesterol or want to lose weight, try to reduce or cut out oils in your cooking. We only use a small amount of oil when cooking, and coconut oil in desserts for a treat, but we are under no illusion that they are a healthy addition.

OVEN TEMPERATURES

All the electric oven temperatures given in our recipes are for a conventional oven. If using a fan oven, decrease them by 20°C/35°F.

PEPPERMINT OIL

This is derived from the peppermint plant and adds a really distinctive minty flavour to any dessert or dish. (And it's also great for clearing up your sinuses!) It's very strong, so use it very sparingly – one drop at a time. It is usually available in health food stores or in the baking section of the supermarket. Try to buy a quality oil.

POLENTA FLOUR

Polenta flour is coarsely ground yellow cornmeal. It gets its name because it's used to make polenta, a thick porridge-like dish from Italy. Cornflour and cornmeal are usually more finely ground and are often not as sweet nor made with yellow corn. If you can't get polenta flour, replace it with medium or coarse ground cornmeal or cornflour.

QUINOA

Quinoa is a staple at this stage. It's a mighty little seed that is often mistaken for a grain. Like rice you cook it by volume (in the ration 2:1 liquid-to-grain), so once you've measured out the amount specified in the recipe, see how far up it comes in a mug or measuring jug before putting it into a medium-size saucepan. Then, using the same mug or jug, measure out twice that volume of water or stock and add it to the quinoa with a pinch of salt. Bring to the boil, then reduce the heat to the lowest setting, cover, and cook until all the water has been absorbed (about 15–20 minutes). Remove from the heat and leave to stand, still covered, for 5 minutes – this helps it puff right up and become much softer. You'll know it's ready when the grains have 'popped' and the germ is exposed and will have a little 'tail'!

RENNET

Most commercial cheeses are made using vegetarian rennet. Parmesan is one of the few cheeses that uses animal rennet, but there are plenty of veggie versions of that on the market. Use a hard aged Cheddar if you can't find a veggie Parmesan.

RICE

We eat plenty of rice, always brown. Steve likes brown basmati, as it's usually fluffier; Dave likes short-grain brown rice for its nutty taste. Brown takes a little longer to cook, but is much higher in fibre and provides a much slower release of energy. Rinse the rice in cold water, using a sieve. Put it into a saucepan and cover with at least twice the amount of water (by volume – so if you used a cup to measure out the rice, add two cups of water). Put the lid on and bring to the boil. Then turn the heat down to a very gentle simmer and cook with the lid on till nearly all the water has evaporated (about 30 minutes). Never let the pot dry out – if it does and the rice is not yet cooked, simply add more water. You will know that the rice is cooked when the grains are completely clear of any white dot. They should be soft and tender.

'SEAWEED: Seaweed is a total superfood, loaded with minerals and trace elements. As it is a sea veg it has levels of nutrition you don't get in veg grown in soil. According to a study reported in the *British Journal of Nutrition*, arame and wakame are high in iron, calcium, folate and magnesium, while also containing lots of B vitamins. We usually add arame to salads, dulse and kombu to soups and stews, and use nori for sushi.'

Spice
Tumeric
Ground Cinnamon
Mild Chilli Powder
Ground Ginger
Curry Powder
Smoked Paprika
Cumin
Cardamon
Chilli flakes
Bay leaves
Sweet Paprika

SALT

In the HP kitchens we use an unrefined grey Atlantic sea salt, and at home we tend to use Irish Atlantic sea salt or Maldon sea salt.

SEAWEED

Seaweed is a total superfood, loaded with minerals and trace elements. As it is a sea veg it has levels of nutrition you don't get in veg grown in soil. According to a study reported in the *British Journal of Nutrition*, arame and wakame are high in iron, calcium, folate and magnesium, while also containing lots of B vitamins. We usually add arame to salads, dulse and kombu to soups and stews, and use nori for sushi.

SPIRULINA

A superfood blue-green algae sea veg that is one of the oldest life forms on the planet and one of the most concentrated food sources too. It is very high in protein, and is also an excellent source of B vitamins and minerals, particularly iron. It is widely available in powder or tablet form from most health food stores. It's used as a health tonic or elixir. Dave uses it in his morning smoothie with his kids. We also sometimes use it to turn things green!

STERILIZING JARS

Put the kettle on to boil. Put the lids and the jars into a saucepan. (We've always used jam jars – as long as you put the lids in before the jars the metal lids absorb the heat and the jars don't crack.) Once the kettle is boiled, pour in the water, covering the lids and jars. Turn the heat to high and boil for a few minutes. If you're nervous about this method, check online for methods using the oven or microwave.

TAMARI

Tamari is a more complex soy sauce that has been aged longer, so has a smoother and rounder taste.

It gives a nice salty flavour to any dish you add it to. It is usually gluten-free, but it's best to check the brand if you are a coeliac, as it isn't always.

TEMPEH

We use tempeh quite a bit, usually in Asian-style stir-fry dishes or easy dinners. Tempeh is like tofu's older brother. It is a fermented soya bean block that has a meaty texture and is easy to get lots of flavour into. It has much more fibre and protein than tofu, and being fermented it usually contains lots of healthy bacteria for your gut. It is usually not as readily available as tofu, but try the chill cabinet in your local Asian shop.

VANILLA FLAVOURING

There is quite a difference between vanilla essence and vanilla extract. Vanilla essence is a lot cheaper and is chemically made, but to get the full hit of flavour you need to use a bit more of it. Vanilla extract is purer and more concentrated and more expensive. But because it's concentrated, you don't need to use as much of it. In our recipes we specify vanilla extract.

VEGETABLE PREPARATION

In our recipes you should assume vegetables are unpeeled unless we say otherwise. As most of the nutrients are in the skin, we recommend giving the vegetables a good wash and leaving the skin on. When using leeks, use the full leek including the green tops, not just the white part.

WHOLE-FOOD DIET

By 'whole food' we mean unrefined plant food, so any fruit, veg, beans or legumes (lentil, chickpea, etc.), or wholegrain (brown rice, etc.). A whole-food plant-based diet is a diet based around these foods. It's not an all or nothing thing, so if you eat meat or fish or some treats, that's fine. To get the benefits of all the great stuff in whole foods, just make sure a good proportion of your diet is made up of whole plant foods!

INDEX

THANKS

We thought our second book would be a stroll in the park, but it was not the case! Yet again, we have relied on a huge amount of people to help us get this one over the line.

First, thanks to our families for putting up with the extra workload while we were writing this book. Thanks to Justyna, May and Theo; Janet, Elsie and Issy. Special thanks to Janet for your fantastic section on feeding kids healthier food – you really walk the talk! Thanks to Mum and Dad, Donal and Ismay, for reading, tasting and for always being there when we need support (and for letting us shoot the book in your house); to Darragh for being the engine in the HP and as much a part of this story as we are – we are very proud to be your bro; to Mark for your help and support from a distance and for your clear brotherly perspective; and to our newest family member (as of September 2015), Darragh's wife Yeşim, for your calm presence, for trialing so many recipes and for somehow turning our rough notes into something coherent that we could send to Penguin!

Thanks to all the great recipe testers who helped us tweak and refine these recipes in their intended environment – home kitchens. Everyone was so up for it, so encouraging and supportive, and so meticulous in their approach and detailed in their feedback, and we are truly indebted to you all. So, to Eileen Woods; Silvie Cahill and her family; Danica Murphy; Killian Fitzgerald, Lucas and Bee; Leonard O'Kelly; Tess and Kelvin (and Finlay and Cuan); Susan Grogan and the Grogan clan; Wendy Richard and Ruth Coburn; Fiona Manning; Lisa Fawsitt; Mellen Fawsitt (Mel, thanks for your great recipe too!); John Shiel (thanks for your friendship and for urging us to include a BBQ section – the BBQ recipes are most definitely dedicated to you!). A special thanks to Maura Winston and Kevin Hogan for letting us use your house for a month while we came up with most of these recipes.

Thanks to Michael Emberley and Mel Fitzpatrick, Larry O'Loughlin, Paul Byrne, Denis Gray, Danica and Ken Murphy for your contributions, and to Amory Schwartz and Auveen Lush for your pieces about our Happy Heart Course. You guys have kept us going, so thanks for being such wonderful friends and for your input.

Thanks to the fantastic Sarah Fraser in Penguin's art department for putting so much into this project. From styling shots to the final design, your great eye for beauty and detail has been invaluable in creating this lovely book. You are a pleasure to work with and do a wonderful job. Thanks also to Gail Jones for assisting with the design. A massive shout-out to John Hamilton for overseeing and driving on this project and for keeping a watchful eye on it – you are brill and a total dude!

Thanks to Alistair Richardson for doing such an amazing photography job. You managed to capture our food and life and you are just going from strength to strength. Thank you for always going the extra mile. Also to Seánie Cahill for shooting the cover and supplementary photography throughout the book – thanks for working so closely with us and for your friendship. You are a great man! Thanks to our dear friend and neighbour Mark Lawlor, and also to Elizabeth Shanks, for kindly allowing us to shoot on your properties! A special thanks to Joanne Murphy and Terry for lending us some of your lovely boards and crockery for the photo shoot – you guys rock! Thanks to Simon Pratt and Monique not just for lending us lots of props for the shoot, but also for all the guidance and support over the years. A special thanks to Geoffrey Healy, for lending us his soulful beautiful pottery (pages 55, 95, 129, 202, 205 and 237). Thanks also for props to Claire Brennan, Mary B Deevy, Kieran Brennan (who made the bowl on page 80) and Gillian McConnell (who made the bowl on pages 97 and 159). And a very special thanks to Niamh Fitzsimons, prop manager and kitchen porter for the shoot, for your calmness, good humour and Trojan work.

At Penguin, thanks to our wonderful editor, Patricia Deevy, for putting your heart into this project too. You are amazing and we love you dearly: thanks for all your support and guidance and your incredible work ethic – you rock! Thanks to Michael McLoughlin, Patricia McVeigh, Cliona Lewis, Brian Walker and all the team in Penguin Ireland. In London, thanks to Joanna Prior for your support and always being so lovely to deal with. Also at 80 Strand, thanks to James Blackman, Sara Granger, Keith Taylor, Poppy North, Celeste Ward-Best, Sara D'Arcy, Sam Fanaken, Catherine Wood and Nicky Palmer, all of whom have been vital in helping us in different ways.

Thanks also to Annie Lee for all your top-class copy-editing, you are a pleasure to work with as always and have an amazing eye for detail. Thanks to Carla Bredin from Wild Healthy, nutritionist on our Happy Heart Course, for reading the health section and reassuring us that we were not writing gobbledygook!

Thanks to our dear friend Tamsin English for getting the whole process started – this would not have happened without you. We love you dearly! And thanks to our agents, Faith O'Grady and Eavan Kenny, you guys are brill and a pleasure to work with.

Next, thanks to the fantastic team that makes the Happy Pear what it is. Without you there would be no Happy Pear. Thanks to our cousin Naomi Smith for putting your heart and soul into the HP and for keeping everything running when we are off chasing our next shiny project! To Siobhán Hanley, our woman-of-all-trades, for being so supportive, caring and amazing over the years; to Juan, our head chef, for your commitment, wonderful manner and great contribution to this book; to Dorene for ten years' service in the trenches, for being such a huge influence on how we cook, for helping to make the HP kitchen what it is and for testing recipes for this book; to Clare for your inspired recipes, for your incredible palette and natural brilliance in the kitchen; to Gong Ping, He Qiang, Giuliano Santos and Diego Abreu for your incredible hard work and bringing lots of new food cultures and flavours to our kitchen; to Jennifer Rooney, our head baker, for recipe-testing and for always being so diligent and positive and ready to embrace every crazy idea we have; to Emily Tebbit, the other half of our baking duo, for your hard work and loyalty – it's been such a pleasure watching you grow and develop over the five years since you started with us during your work experience in school. A special thanks to Kevin Mulvaney for being our right-hand man on this project, trialing recipes, organizing so much of the ingredients and throwing yourself into this project. Go Kev!

Thanks to Paul Grimes and Shane Murphy, the coffee maestros – you are both legends; to Namey D, Raj, Jack, Anto, Yuri, Cathy, Joe and Michael, Fiona, tall Mike, Arron, Siobhán Whelan, Santo Christiano, Rob, Kruk, Serene, Paul Deighton (aka 'Aussie Paul'), Tess Carr (our night-time restaurant manager, pictured on page 240), and all the team; to the wonderful Sarah Dunne for working so closely with us, for your commitment, amazing work ethic and capacity to deal with chaos and us; to Szymon for all your mighty contribution on the farm and in our new Pear Factory – you are a powerful man; to Anne Crotty for running such a tight ship on our lovely pesto team. Thanks to Alan Smith (head elder) – your friendship, guidance and support with all things business, branding, and more, has been invaluable. Thanks to all our elders – Ashley Glover, Rod Large, Aidan O Byrne and Amory Schwarz, you guys are amazing. Thanks to all our lovely suppliers – thanks for your great produce and service, you are all central to what we do.

Finally, thanks to the people of our home-town of Greystones and our extended community – thank you for your support. Without it there would be no Happy Pear!

Dave & Steve xx

#eatmoreveg